THE ENVIRONMENT IN CRISIS
PROGRESSIVE PERSPECTIVES FROM *DOLLARS & SENSE*

Third edition

Edited by Daniel Fireside, Toussaint Losier, Adria Scharf, Thad Williamson, and the *Dollars & Sense* Collective

The Environment in Crisis
Progressive Perspectives from *Dollars & Sense*

Edited by Daniel Fireside, Toussaint Losier, Adria Scharf, Thad Williamson, and the *Dollars & Sense* Collective

ISBN: 1-878585-51-7

Published by:
Dollars & Sense
Economic Affairs Bureau, Inc.
29 Winter Street
Boston, MA 02108
Phone: (617) 447-2177
Fax: (617) 447-2179
E-mail: dollars@dollarsandsense.org
Web: www.dollarsandsense.org

The Environment in Crisis is edited by the *Dollars & Sense* Collective, which also publishes *Dollars & Sense* magazine and *Real World Macro*, *Real World Micro*, *The Wealth Inequality Reader*, *Real World Globalization*, *Real World Banking*, *Introduction to Political Economy*, *Unlevel Playing Fields: Understanding Wage Inequality and Discrimination*, *Grassroots Journalism*, and *Striking a Balance*. For subscription information and an updated book catalog, please visit www.dollarsandsense.org.

Cover Design: Nick Thorkelson
Production: Alyssa Hassan

Manufactured by Capital City Press
Printed in U.S.A.

® GCIU 196

CONTENTS

Chapter 5: Environmental Protection and the Developing World

Chapter 6: Changing the System, Changing How We Live

CHAPTER 1

VALUING THE ENVIRONMENT IN ECONOMIC THEORY

THE GROWTH CONSENSUS UNRAVELS

JONATHAN ROWE

July/August 1999*

Economics has been called the dismal science, but beneath its gray exterior is a system of belief worthy of Pollyanna.

Yes, economists manage to see a dark cloud in every silver lining. Downturn follows uptick, and inflation rears its ugly head. But there's a story within that story—a gauzy romance, a lyric ode to Stuff. It's built into the language. A thing produced is called a "good," for example, no questions asked. The word is more than just a term of art. It suggests the automatic benediction which economics bestows upon commodities of any kind.

By the same token, an activity for sale is called a "service." In conventional economics there are no "dis-services," no actions that might be better left undone. The bank that gouges you with ATM fees, the lawyer who runs up the bill—such things are "services" so long as someone pays. If a friend or neighbor fixes your plumbing for free, it's not a "service" and so it doesn't count.

The sum total of these products and activities is called the Gross Domestic Product, or GDP. If the GDP is greater this year than last, then the result is called

*Dates denote when the article appeared in *Dollars & Sense* magazine.

"growth." There is no bad GDP and no bad growth; economics does not even have a word for such a thing. It does have a word for less growth. In such a case, economists say growth is "sluggish" and the economy is in "recession." No matter what is growing—more payments to doctors because of worsening health, more toxic cleanup—so long as there is more of it, then the economic mind declares it "good."

This purports to be "objective science." In reality it is a rhetorical construct with the value judgments built in, and this rhetoric has been the basis of economic debate in the United States for the last half century at least. True, people have disagreed over how best to promote a rising GDP. Liberals generally wanted to use government more, conservatives less. But regarding the beneficence of a rising GDP, there has been little debate at all.

If anything, the Left traditionally has believed in growth with even greater fervor than the Right. It was John Maynard Keynes, after all, who devised the growth-boosting mechanisms of macroeconomic policy to combat the Depression of the 1930s; it was Keynesians who embraced these strategies after the War and turned the GDP into a totem. There's no point in seeking a bigger pie to redistribute to the poor, if you don't believe the expanding pie is desirable in the first place.

Today, however, the growth consensus is starting to unravel across the political spectrum and in ways that are both obvious and subtle. The issue is no longer just the impact of growth upon the environment—the toxic impacts of industry and the like. It now goes deeper, to what growth actually consists of and what it means in people's lives. The things economists call "goods" and "services" increasingly don't strike people as such. There is a growing disconnect between the way people experience growth and the way the policy establishment talks about it, and this gap is becoming an unspoken subtext to much of American political life.

The group most commonly associated with an antigrowth stance is environmentalists, of course. To be sure, one faction, the environmental economists, is trying to put green new wine into the old bottles of economic thought. If we would just make people pay the "true" cost of, say, the gasoline they burn, through the tax system for example, then the market would do the rest. We'd have benign, less-polluting growth, they say, perhaps even more than now. But the core of the environmental movement remains deeply suspicious of the growth ethos, and probably would be even if the environmental impacts somehow could be lessened.

In the middle are suburbanites who applaud growth in the abstract, but oppose the particular manifestations they see around them—the traffic, sprawl and crowded schools. On the Right, meanwhile, an anti-growth politics is arising practically unnoticed. When social conservatives denounce gambling, pornography, or sex and violence in the media, they are talking about specific instances of the growth that their political leaders rhapsodize on other days.

Environmentalists have been like social conservatives in one key respect. They have been moralistic regarding growth, often scolding people for enjoying themselves at the expense of future generations and the earth. Their concern is valid, up to a point—the consumer culture does promote the time horizon of a five year old. But politically it is not the most promising line of attack, and conceptually it concedes too much ground. To moralize about consumption as they do is to accept the conventional premise that it really is something chosen—an enjoyable form of self-indulgence that has unfortunate consequences for the earth.

That's "consumption" in the common parlance—the sport utility vehicle loading up at Wal-Mart, the stuff piling up in the basement and garage. But increasingly that's not what people actually experience, nor is it what the term really means. In economics, consumption means everything people spend money on, pleasurable or not. Wal-Mart is just one dimension of a much larger and increasingly unpleasant whole. The lawyers' fees for the house settlement or divorce; the repair work on the car after it was rear-ended; the cancer treatments for the uncle who was a three-pack-a-day smoker; the stress medications and weight loss regimens—all these and more are "consumption." They all go into the GDP.

Cancer treatments and lawyer's fees are not what come to mind when environmentalists lament the nation's excess consumption, or for that matter when economists applaud America's "consumers" for keeping the world economy afloat. Yet increasingly such things are what consumption actually consists of in the economy today. More and more, it consists not of pleasurable things that people choose, but rather of things that most people would gladly do without.

Much consumption today is addictive, for example. Millions of Americans are engaged in a grim daily struggle with themselves to do less of it. They want to eat less, drink less, smoke less, gamble less, talk less on the telephone—do less buying, period. Yet economic reasoning declares as growth and progress, that which people themselves regard as a tyrannical affliction.

Economists resist this reality of a divided self, because it would complicate their models beyond repair. They cling instead to an 18th century model of human psychology—the "rational" and self-interested man—which assumes those complexities away. As David McClelland, the Harvard psychologist, once put it, economists "haven't even discovered Freud, let alone Abraham Maslow." (They also haven't discovered the Apostle Paul, who lamented that "the good that I would I do not, but the evil that I would not, that I do.")

Then too there's the mounting expenditure that sellers foist upon people through machination and deceit. People don't choose to pay for the corrupt campaign finance system or for bloated executive pay packages. The cost of these is hidden in the prices that we pay at the store. As I write this, the *Washington Post* is reporting that Microsoft has hired Ralph Reed, former head of the Christian Coalition, and Grover Norquist, a right-wing polemicist, as lobbyists in Washington. When I bought this computer with Windows 95, Bill Gates never asked me whether I wanted to help support a bunch of Beltway operators like these.

This is compulsory consumption, not choice, and the economy is rife with it today. People don't choose to pay some $40 billion a year in telemarketing fraud.

They don't choose to pay 32% more for prescription drugs than do people in Canada. ("Free trade" means that corporations are free to buy their labor and materials in other countries, but ordinary Americans aren't equally free to do their shopping there.) For that matter, people don't choose to spend $25 and up for inkjet printer cartridges. The manufacturers design the printers to make money on the cartridges because, as the *Wall Street Journal* put it, that's "where the big profit margins are."

Yet another category of consumption that most people would gladly do without arises from the need to deal with the offshoots and implications of growth. Bottled water has become a multibillion dollar business in the United States because people don't trust what comes from the tap. There's a growing market for sound insulation and double-pane windows because the economy produces so much noise. A wide array of physical and social stresses arise from the activities that get lumped into the euphemistic term "growth."

The economy in such cases doesn't solve problems so much as create new problems that require more expenditure to solve. Food is supposed to sustain people, for example. But today the dis-economies of eating sustain the GDP instead. The food industry spends some $21 billion a year on advertising to entice people to eat food they don't need. Not coincidentally there's now a $32 billion diet and weight loss industry to help people take off the pounds that inevitably result. When that doesn't work, which is often, there is always the vacuum pump or knife. There were some 110,000 liposuctions in the United States last year; at five pounds each that's some 275 tons of flab up the tube.

It is a grueling cycle of indulgence and repentance, binge and purge. Yet each stage of this miserable experience, viewed through the pollyanic lens of economics, becomes growth and therefore good. The problem here goes far beyond the old critique of how the consumer culture cultivates feelings of inadequacy, lack and need so people will buy and buy again. Now this culture actually makes life worse, in order to sell solutions that purport to make it better.

Traffic shows this syndrome in a finely developed form. First we build sprawling suburbs so people need a car to go almost anywhere. The resulting long commutes are daily torture but help build up the GDP. Americans spend some $5 billion a year in gasoline alone while they sit in traffic and go nowhere. As the price of gas increases this growth sector will expand.

Commerce deplores a vacuum, and the exasperating hours in the car have spawned a booming subeconomy of relaxation tapes, cell phones, even special bibs. Billboards have 1-800 numbers so commuters can shop while they stew. Talk radio thrives on traffic-bound commuters, which accounts for some of the contentious, get-out-of-my-face tone. The traffic also helps sustain a $130 billion a year car wreck industry; and if Gates succeeds in getting computers into cars, that sector should get a major boost.

The health implications also are good for growth. Los Angeles, which has the worst traffic in the nation, also leads—if that's the word—in hospital admissions due to respiratory ailments. The resulting medical bills go into the GDP. And while Americans sit in traffic they aren't walking or getting exercise. More likely they are entertaining themselves orally with a glazed donut or a Big Mac, which helps explain why the portion of middle-aged Americans who are clinically obese has doubled since the 1960s.

C. Everett Koop, the former Surgeon General, estimates that some 70% of the nation's medical expenses are lifestyle induced. Yet the same lifestyle that promotes disease also produces a rising GDP. (Keynes observed that traditional virtues like thrift are bad for growth; now it appears that health is bad for growth too.) We literally are growing ourselves sick, and this puts a grim new twist on the economic doctrine of "complementary goods," which describes the way new products tend to spawn a host of others. The automobile gave rise to car wash franchises, drive-in restaurants, fuzz busters, tire dumps, and so forth. Television produced an antenna industry, VCRs, soap magazines, ad infinitum. The texts present this phenomenon as the wondrous perpetual motion machine of the market—goods beget more goods. But now the machine is producing complementary ills and collateral damages instead.

Suggestive of this new dynamic is a pesticide plant in Richmond, California, which is owned by a transnational corporation that also makes the breast cancer drug tamoxifen. Many researchers believe that pesticides, and the toxins created in the production of them, play a role in breast cancer. "It's a pretty good deal," a local physician told the *East Bay Express*, a Bay Area weekly. "First you cause the cancer, then you profit from curing it." Both the alleged cause and cure make the GDP go up, and this syndrome has become a central dynamic of growth in the U.S. today.

Mainstream economists would argue that this is all beside the point. If people didn't have to spend money on such things as commuting or medical costs, they'd simply spend it on something else, they say. Growth would be the same or even greater, so the actual content of growth should be of little concern to those who promote it. That view holds sway in the nation's policy councils; as a result we try continually to grow our way out of problems, when increasingly we are growing our way in.

To the extent conventional economics has raised an eyebrow at growth, it has done so mainly through the concept of "externalities". These are negative side effects suffered by those not party to a transaction between a buyer and a seller. Man buys car, car pollutes air, others suffer that "externality." As the language implies, anything outside the original transaction is deemed secondary, a subordinate reality, and therefore easily overlooked. More, the effects upon buyer and seller—the "internalities" one might say—are assumed to be good.

Today, however, that mental schema is collapsing. Externalities are starting to overwhelm internalities. A single jet ski can cause more misery for the people who reside by a lake, than it gives pleasure to the person riding it.

More importantly, and as just discussed, internalities themselves are coming into question, and with them the assumption of choice, which is the moral linchpin of market thought.

If people choose what they buy, as market theory posits, then—externalities aside—the sum total of all their buying must be the greatest good of all. That's the ideology behind the GDP. But if people don't always choose, then the model starts to fall apart, which is what is happening today. The practical implications are obvious. If growth consists increasingly of problems rather than solutions, then scolding people for consuming too much is barking up the wrong tree. It is possible to talk instead about ridding our lives of what we don't want as well as forsaking what we do want—or think we want.

Politically this is a more promising path. But to where? The economy may be turning into a kind of round robin of difficulty and affliction, but we are all tied to the game. The sickness industry employs a lot of people, as do ad agencies and trash haulers. The fastest-growing occupations in the country include debt collectors and prison guards. What would we do without our problems and dysfunctions?

The problem is especially acute for those at the bottom of the income scale who have not shared much in the apparent prosperity. For them, a bigger piece of a bad pie might be better than none.

This is the economic conundrum of our age. No one has more than pieces of an answer, but it helps to see that much growth today is really an optical illusion created by accounting tricks. The official tally ignores totally the cost side of the growth ledger—the toll of traffic upon our time and health for example. In fact, it actually counts such costs as growth and gain. By the same token, the official tally ignores the economic contributions of the natural environment and the social structure; so that the more the economy destroys these, and puts commoditized substitutes in their places, the more the experts say the economy has "grown." Pollute the lakes and oceans so that people have to join private swim clubs and the economy grows. Erode the social infrastructure of community so people have to buy services from the market instead of getting help from their neighbors, and it grows some more. The real economy—the one that sustains us—has diminished. All that has grown is the need to buy commoditized substitutes for things we used to have for free.

So one might rephrase the question thus: how do we achieve real growth, as opposed to the statistical illusion that passes for growth today? Four decades ago, John Kenneth Galbraith argued in *The Affluent Society* that conventional economic reasoning is rapidly becoming obsolete. An economics based upon scarcity simply doesn't work in an economy of hyper-abundance, he said. If it takes a $200 billion (today) advertising industry to maintain what economists quaintly call "demand," then perhaps that demand isn't as urgent as conventional theory posits. Perhaps it's not even demand in any sane meaning of the word.

Galbraith argued that genuine economy called for shifting some resources from consumption that needs to be prodded, to needs which are indisputably great: schools, parks, older people, the inner cities and the like. For this he was skewered as a proto-socialist. Yet today the case is even stronger, as advertisers worm into virtually every waking moment in a desperate effort to keep the growth machine on track.

Galbraith was arguing for a larger public sector. But that brings dysfunctions of its own, such as bureaucracy; and it depends upon an enlarging private sector as a fiscal base to begin with. Today we need to go further, and establish new ground rules for the economy, so that it produces more genuine growth on its own. We also need to find ways to revive the nonmarket economy of informal community exchange, so that people do not need money to meet every single life need.

In the first category, environmental fiscal policy can help. While the corporate world has flogged workers to be more productive, resources such as petroleum have been in effect loafing on the job. If we used these more efficiently the result could be jobs and growth, even in conventional terms, with less environmental pollution. If we used land more efficiently—that is, reduced urban sprawl—the social and environmental gains would be great.

Another ground rule is the corporate charter laws. We need to restore these to their original purpose: to keep large business organizations within the compass of the common good. But such shifts can do only so much. More efficient cars might simply encourage more traffic, for example. Cheap renewable power for electronic devices could encourage more noise. In other words, the answer won't just be a more efficient version of what we do now. Sooner or later we'll need different ways of thinking about work and growth and how we allocate the means of life.

This is where the social economy comes in, the informal exchange between neighbors and friends. There are some promising trends. One is the return to the traditional village model in housing. Structure does affect content. When houses are close together, and people can walk to stores and work, it encourages the spontaneous social interaction that nurtures real community. New local currencies, such as Time Dollars, provide a kind of lattice work upon which informal nonmarket exchange can take root and grow.

Changes like these are off the grid of economics as conventionally defined. It took centuries for the market to emerge from the stagnation of feudalism. The next organizing principle, whatever it is, most likely will emerge slowly as well. This much we can say with certainty. As the market hurdles towards multiple implosions, social and environmental as well as financial, it is just possible that the economics profession is going to have to do what it constantly lectures the rest of us to do: adjust to new realities and show a willingness to change.

ECOLOGICAL FOOTPRINTS

DAVID HOLTZMAN

July/August 1999

What is to blame for global warming, depleting fossil fuels, and other environmental problems? Overpopulated Third World countries with lax environmental standards, as the Heritage Foundation and other conservative think tanks assert, or overconsuming First World economies, as most environmentalists maintain?

Mathis Wackernagel and William Rees, two community planners at the University of British Columbia in Canada, developed an innovative way to answer this question in the 1996 book *The Ecological Footprint.* Their statistical measure—what they call an ecological footprint—reveals the impact each country has on the world's resources. Not surprisingly, "modern" economies, such as the United States, have the largest ecological footprints. These economies require far more land, energy, and water, and emit much more of the carbon dioxide that is so harmful to people's health and the atmosphere, than do poorer nations, even though poor nations are home to most of the world's population.

The ecological footprint measures the resources consumed by a community or a nation, whether they come from the community's backyard or around the globe. Earlier studies had determined a community or nation's "carrying capacity"—the number of people a society can support before it loses its ability to support itself. Wackernagel and Rees' innovation adds in richer countries' use of trade and technology to import resources they don't possess.

Wackernagel and Rees ask how many hectares or acres are needed per person to support a nation's consumption of food, housing, transportation, consumer goods, and services. They calculate how much fossil energy use, land degradation, and garden, crop, pasture, and forest space it takes to produce all the consumers buy.

For example, Wackernagel and Rees determined that Vancouver, British Columbia, their home, runs a large "ecological deficit" with the rest of the world. As they calculate it, Vancouver needs an area 19 times larger than its 4,000 square kilometers to support the food production, forest products, and energy consumption of the region.

Compared globally, the Wackernagel and Rees results are stunning. Based on 1991 figures, the U.S. ecological footprint was 5.1 hectares per person, or over 12.5 acres. In contrast, each resident of India, which has a population three times the size of the United States, requires 0.4 hectares or just over two acres to maintain his or her livelihood per year.

The implications of these ecological footprints for world development are profoundly disturbing. For instance, for everyone on Earth to enjoy the ecological standards of average residents in Canada and the United States, an additional planet or two might be necessary. And while the material wealth of people in the rich countries increased during the 20th century, the First World exploited so much space and resources in the process that little is left for poor countries hoping to obtain a similar standard of living in the same manner.

To sustain these inequitable ecological footprints, most rich countries run large ecological deficits with the rest of the world. The United States, one of the most land-rich modern economies, is one of the few exceptions.

If the ecological marks left by all the world's people are to be distributed more equitably, then Americans, Canadians, and other residents of wealthy countries are going to have to change their habits radically. A modest first step in that direction would be to require that the industries and governments that drive the world economy include an analysis of their impacts on the environment, or ecological footprint, in their economic forecasts.

Resources: Mathis Wackernagel and William Rees, *Our Ecological Footprint: Reducing Human Impact on the Earth* (New Society Publishers, 1996); *www.wri.org/data/matflows.* To determine your own ecological footprint, visit *www.myfootprint.org.*

IS THE U.S. MAKING PROGRESS?

UNLIKE THE GDP, A NEW MEASURE SAYS "NO"

MARC BRESLOW

March/April 1996

Suppose a factory in your community has been producing valuable chemicals for several decades. It employs hundreds of workers, purchases materials and services from nearby towns, and yields high profits. Then inspectors for the Environmental Protection Agency discover that the factory owners have been dumping hazardous wastes onto the company's land, polluting the local water supply. Under the federal "Superfund" law, EPA orders a cleanup and tries to make the company pay for the damages. In turn, the company resists the EPA in court.

What do these events mean for society? Contrary to common sense, all are counted as positive by the nation's primary measure of economic output, Gross Domestic Product, or GDP. This indicator includes not only the dollar value of constructing the factory, paying wages to employees, and generating profits for the owners—but also the millions of dollars spent to clean up toxic wastes and to restore the purity of the water supply. GDP even includes the health care expenses of anyone who contracts cancer or other illnesses from drinking contaminated water. And, the money spent by EPA to regulate the polluter, and by the company on lawyers and experts to defend itself against regulation, both add to the official measure of national output.

Not only does the GDP count as "progress" many things that do not deserve the label, but it fails to count items that genuinely improve national welfare. Try another example. You and your domestic partner Jean are both working full-time, while your three-year-old daughter Kim is in day care 40 hours a week, at a cost of $10,000 a year. Both Jean and you are exhausted by the hectic schedule of going to work, picking Kim up from her center, and then caring for her as soon as you get home. You feel guilty about how much time Kim is in an institutional setting, and wish you could be with her more. On the plus side, both your salaries and the day care expenses add to the nation's GDP.

But then an amazing thing happens. The company that you work for, and the government agency where Jean works, both decide to allow part-time work. You cut back to three days a week, Jean cuts back to four days, and you keep Kim in day care for three days. Kim is happier, you enjoy being with her more, both you and Jean have more free time, and your relationship improves. Money is tighter, but you can still pay the bills.

A happy ending? Yes, except that the economic statisticians will hate you. By cutting your wages, and by reducing your payments to the day care center, you have harmed the GDP. And, the extra two days a week that you and Jean spend caring for Kim yourselves count for nothing, since no one is paying you to do it.

These are not extreme examples. GDP, the primary method by which economic progress is measured in the United States and throughout the world, is a highly misleading index. While the adjective "economic" could be viewed as a tipoff that "progress" includes many other things, in practice GDP is often treated as the sole measure of how human welfare is changing.

Even if its meaning is limited to the value of economic output, GDP is fatally flawed. First, as the child care example shows, GDP rises when unpaid household labor is replaced by paid wage labor, even if real "output" has not changed. Second, GDP fails to note that as production rises annually, we are depleting the earth's stocks of fossil fuels, minerals, forests, wetlands, and fish. Unlike business firms, which subtract "depreciation" of their equipment and buildings from annual income, the GDP makes no adjustment for depletion of natural resources.

When GDP's purpose is extended to measuring human welfare, it has even less relevance, since it fails to distinguish between desirable output ("goods") and undesirable output ("bads"). As the pollution example demonstrates, the costs of controlling environmental damages from production, and of repairing our health once the by-products of production have harmed it, add to the GDP no differently than do the food, clothing, and entertainment that we actually get pleasure from consuming.

GDP also fails to account for how production and consumption create environmental problems that threaten future generations, such as global warming and destruction of the ozone layer. And it ignores the worsening of social problems in modern-day America, such as inequality, crime, and loss of leisure time.

REDEFINING PROGRESS

These deficiencies in the "national income" accounts of the United States and other nations have been critiqued by environmentalists, feminists, and those who see social development faltering even as the GDP grows. The United Nations Development Program (UNDP), for example, has for years modified GDP scores by examining the health and educational status of each nation's population, deriving a "Human Development Index."

Recently the group "Redefining Progress," based in San Francisco, created its own alternative to GDP, called the "Genuine Progress Indicator," or GPI. According to Clifford Cobb, Ted Halstead, and Jonathan Rowe, the authors of the group's study:

> Much of what we now call growth or GDP is really just one of three things in disguise: fixing blunders from the past, borrowing resources from the future, or shifting functions from the traditional realm of household and community to the realm of the monetized economy.

While the GPI rose somewhat between 1950 and the early 1970s, it has been falling steadily since then. By 1994 the GPI was 26% lower than it had been in 1973. Since the U.S. population has been growing, what really matters is "progress" per person, which the GPI measures as having fallen by an astounding 42% since 1970!

These figures are consistent with wage and productivity trends that show economic welfare, measured by workers' paychecks, falling since the same year. But the 42% drop is far more severe than the decline in wages. If the GPI accurately reflects reality, then the U.S. economy must be in a dramatic decline.

Upon closer examination, most of Redefining Progress' adjustments to the GDP are based on depletion of natural resources and long-term damage to the environment. So while the welfare of the current generation of Americans has stagnated, but perhaps not dropped greatly, the GPI indicates that we are severely compromising the ability of future generations to enjoy the fruits of the earth.

Many experts will question details of how the GPI was constructed, and will not accept the specifics of their numbers. But there is widespread agreement that Redefining Progress' effort to construct an alternative to the GDP is well-founded. Hundreds of economists, including such mainstream figures as Nobel Laureate Herbert Simon and former president of the American Economics Association Robert Eisner, have called for new measures of economic progress.

INEQUALITY, UNDEREMPLOYMENT, AND OVERWORK

The conventional GDP is a combination of three main elements: consumption, meaning the food, clothing, housing and other expenses of all individuals in the United States; investment by business in items such as machinery and buildings; and spending by government bodies on items such as roads, schools, and the military.

The new GPI breaks each of these elements down more specifically, looking at whether particular expenses are "goods" or "bads." But it still begins with consumption, which increased by an impressive 55%, or $6,200, per person between 1970 and 1994 (all figures in 1994 inflation-adjusted dollars). If we stopped here, we would, as do true believers in the free market, think that life is pretty rosy in America.

But it is now well known that gains in wealth, income, and therefore consumption have been concentrated in the upper classes in recent decades, while wages have fallen for most people and government has cut the real value of assistance for the poor. For its index of inequality, Redefining Progress uses the share of income received by the lowest-income 20% of the population, which was a meager 3.9% in 1990. Counting inequality as a "bad," the per capita GPI falls by $3,700 due to the drop in this share from 1970 to 1994—canceling out more than half of the gain from higher consumption.

While there is no "objective" means of weighting the harm from inequality, the GPI's adjustment appears to be well justified. Government data shows that between 1970 and 1992 the average incomes of the bottom three-fifths of U.S. households were virtually unchanged. Thus, less than half the population has gained from the large rise in consumption.

The GPI also has downward adjustments for two other results of America's destructive labor market—underemployment and loss of leisure time. In recent decades average unemployment has risen slightly in the United States, but "underemployment"—meaning people who want full-time jobs but can only get part-time work during part or all of the year—has skyrocketed. Redefining Progress uses the average real wage as the basis for valuing this involuntary idleness.

The U.S. economy is causing seemingly contradictory difficulties, since at the same time that underemployment is rising for some people, overwork is rising for most others. Due to the simultaneous demands of paid labor and unpaid child care, leisure time has been falling consistently. Based on research by Laura Leete-Guy and Juliet Schor (author of *The Overworked American*), Redefining Progress estimates that hours of leisure per fully employed member of the workforce fell by an average of more than 100 per year, or two hours per week, from 1969 to 1989.

Clifford Cobb and his co-authors have also made adjustments for other social problems, including the costs of households protecting themselves from crime, of increasing rates of family breakdown, of longer commuting times to work, and of auto accidents. But while these are conceptually important, the authors' methodology makes them small numerically relative to labor market and environmental factors.

In several cases the GPI appears to underestimate social damages. For example, it limits the costs of crime to the value of stolen goods and to spending on locks, burglar alarms and other "defensive" measures. But surely these are only minor parts of the real damage from rising crime and exploding rates of incarceration. There are now more than a million Americans in prison, a figure that has doubled in the past decade. Is not the loss in freedom to these prisoners far more important than the expenses of buying alarm systems? And what about increasing social division, as most people who can afford to do so move out of urban neighborhoods, partially to escape from crime?

DESTROYING THE EARTH

While the GPI may underestimate the social costs of life in modern-day America, it probably overestimates the environmental costs. Redefining Progress asserts that destruction of old-growth forests, elimination of farmland and wetlands, depletion of non-renewable resources (principally oil), destruction of the ozone layer, and global warming are in combination the most important reasons to discard Gross Domestic Product as a measure of progress. The GPI counts these failures to conserve the bounties Mother Earth as subtracting $4,900 per person from the 1994 GDP—much more than the adjustments for rising inequality, loss of leisure time, and higher underemployment combined.

Although resource destruction is accelerating in the United States and worldwide, the GPI indicates that more "traditional" environmental problems—water and air pollution—have not gotten worse in the United States since 1970. In fact, while the costs of water pollution have remained constant, those from air pollution have been cut in half. Redefining Progress estimates that while air quality deteriorated in the United States during the 1950s and 1960s, it began improving by 3% per year in the 1970s, due to the Clean Air Act of 1970.

Perhaps these results are not surprising, given that government policies have been focused on restricting pollution but not on controlling the use of resources. But how should we view our overuse of the earth? Should all of us alive today, who enjoy using our four-wheel drive autos, building houses in the far reaches of suburbia on former farmlands or wetlands, and using our ozone-destroying air conditions, feel guilty that our grandchildren will have less because we have more?

Most economists—including many who consider themselves environmentalists—would disagree with this perspective. They would argue that with each succeeding generation the economy's capacity to produce becomes greater, and levels

TAXES FOR PROGRESS

Having a better statistical measure of progress is a good idea, but by itself will not change the course of industrial civilization. To help accomplish this goal, Redefining Progress proposes that the United States inhibit pollution and resource depletion by placing severe taxes on the use of resources such as energy fuels.

As the World Resources Institute did in its book *Green Fees*, Redefining Progress argues that such taxes would have a dual benefit. First, they would discourage the use of fuels, thereby limiting global warming and acid rain, and conserving resources for our descendants.

Second, the resulting revenues would allow the government to reduce or eliminate its taxation of labor and capital investment. The latter are activities that we wish to encourage, but instead discourage at present by taxing them heavily. Redefining Progress estimates that a tax on resources and pollution in California would bring in sufficient revenues to enable abolishing all other state and local taxes. Such a change could, by reducing the cost of hiring employees and investing in plant and equipment, prove to be a great boon to workers and to real economic growth.

of technology improve, so that human "welfare" can rise even as resources become more scarce.

Take, for example, the depletion of petroleum stocks, which is the largest negative adjustment that Redefining Progress makes to the GDP. There have been scares about declining oil supplies for more than a century, with the most recent being the oil "crises" of 1973 and 1979, when the Organization of Petroleum Exporting Countries (OPEC) sharply raised its prices.

But as new supplies of oil have been discovered throughout the world, OPEC's power has declined, and with it the price of crude oil. Gasoline prices in the United States (adjusted for inflation) are only slightly higher today than they were in 1973.

Many economists, politicians, and perhaps the general public have concluded that there is no reason to worry about the availability of oil supplies for the next generation. But Redefining Progress argues that the failure of prices to rise today is weak evidence for believing that our children and grandchildren will not be faced with true resource scarcities. And Cobb et al. may be right. Since oil supplies are currently abundant, prices will only rise if their owners restrict supply by keeping oil in the ground today, while hoping to sell at higher prices in future decades. But if owners are interested only in short-term profits, then they will fail to conserve oil until a true shortage develops.

To account for potential scarcity, and for the current costs of keeping prices low, the GPI treats oil consumption as a loss to society. The index values this loss at the high price of producing a renewable motor fuel—specifically "gasohol" derived from sugar cane or other organic materials. This is estimated at $75 a barrel (as of 1988)—about five times the current cost of buying crude oil on the world market! With oil consumption constituting a significant fraction of all U.S. spending, the $75 estimate causes a huge downward adjustment to the GDP.

While most environmental analysts would probably agree with making some adjustment for resource scarcity, they would question the magnitude of Redefining Progress' estimate. It is likely that succeeding generations will face rising real oil prices over the next century, but Redefining Progress has not provided evidence to support a dramatic fivefold price rise.

Redefining Progress also makes large subtractions from the GDP to account for global warming, ozone depletion, and the gradual destruction of forests, farmland, and wetlands. While the principle behind this is undeniable, the reliability of their specific calculations is again uncertain. Concerning global warming, the Intergovernmental Panel on Climate Change has forecasted that average worldwide temperatures are likely to rise 2.5 degrees centigrade by the year 2025, and economist William Cline has estimated that this would cause $120 billion annually in losses to society.

Warming is primarily due to releases of carbon dioxide to the atmosphere, and such releases are mainly a function of burning fossil fuels. To account for this, Cobb et al. take the cumulative consumption of oil, coal, and natural gas since 1900 and count $1 per barrel of oil (or its equivalent for coal and gas) as a long-term environmental cost. They make the same adjustment for electricity production from nuclear power plants, in view of the long-term threat from disposal of radioactive wastes. This yields a reduction of $645 billion, or more than one-tenth, to the 1994 Gross Domestic Product(!)—far higher than Cline's research justifies.

Although their numbers are debatable, Redefining Progress has focused our attention on a critical problem, and has begun the necessary process of developing a more meaningful indicator of human welfare—one that would take into account the needs of future generations. As the GPI's authors say, if economists don't like their numbers, then the progression should begin the difficult task of developing better ones. In the meantime, the Genuine Progress Indicator is a serious effort to place values on resource depletion, environmental destruction, the household sector, inequality, and social costs. Even if it is a flawed effort, policymakers would do far better to pay attention to the GPI than to the absurdities of the Gross Domestic Product.

Resources: *The Genuine Progress Indicator: Summary of Data and Methodology*, Clifford Cobb, Ted Halstead, and Jonathan Rowe, Redefining Progress, September 1995; "The Green Revenue Path: For Healthy Growth, Washington Should Tax Resources, Not Labor," Halstead and Rowe, *Washington Post*, September 10, 1995; "If the GDP Is Up, Why Is America Down?" Cobb, Halstead, and Rose, *Atlantic Monthly*, October 1995; *Accounts Overdue: National Resource Depreciation in Costa Rica*, World Resources Institute, December 1991.

PRICING THE PRICELESS
INSIDE THE STRANGE WORLD OF COST-BENEFIT ANALYSIS

The cost-benefit analysis of environmental protection simply does not offer the policy-making panacea its adherents promise.

LISA HEINZERLING AND FRANK ACKERMAN
March/April 2003

How strictly should we regulate arsenic in drinking water? Or carbon dioxide in the atmosphere? Or pesticides in our food? Or oil drilling in scenic places? The list of environmental harms and potential regulatory remedies often appears to be endless. In evaluating a proposed new initiative, how do we know if it is worth doing or not? Is there an objective way to decide how to proceed? Cost-benefit analysis promises to provide the solution—to add up the benefits of a public policy and compare them to the costs.

The costs of protecting health and the environment through pollution control devices and other approaches are, by their very nature, measured in dollars. The other side of the balance, calculating the benefits of life, health, and nature in dollars and cents, is far more problematic. Since there are no natural prices for a healthy environment, cost-benefit analysis creates artificial ones. Researchers, for example, may ask a cross-section of the affected population how much they would pay to preserve or protect something that can't be bought in a store. The average American household is supposedly willing to pay $257 to prevent the extinction of bald eagles, $208 to protect humpback whales, and $80 to protect gray wolves.

Costs and benefits of a policy, however, frequently fall at different times. When the analysis spans a number of years, future costs and benefits are discounted, or treated as equivalent to smaller amounts of money in today's dollars. The case for discounting begins with the observation that money received today is worth a little more than money received in the future. (For example, if the interest rate is 3%, you only need to deposit about $97 today to get $100 next year. Economists would say that, at a 3% discount rate, $100 next year has a present value of $97.) For longer periods of time, or higher discount rates, the effect is magnified. The important issue for environmental policy is whether this logic also applies to outcomes far in the future, and to opportunities—like long life and good health—that are not naturally stated in dollar terms.

Why Cost-Benefit Analysis Doesn't Work

The case for cost-benefit analysis of environmental protection is, at best, wildly optimistic and, at worst, demonstrably wrong. The method simply does not offer the policy-making panacea its adherents promise. In practice, cost-benefit analysis frequently produces false and misleading results. Moreover, there is no quick fix, because these failures are intrinsic to the methodology, appearing whenever it is applied to any complex environmental problem.

It puts dollar figures on values that are not commodities, and have no price.

Artificial prices have been estimated for many benefits of environmental regulation. Preventing retardation due to childhood lead poisoning comes in at about $9,000 per lost IQ point. Saving a life is ostensibly worth $6.3 million. But what can it mean to say that one life is worth $6.3 million? You cannot buy the right to kill someone for $6.3 million, nor for any other price. If analysts calculated the value of life itself by asking people what it is worth to them (the most common method of valuation of other environmental benefits), the answer would be infinite. The standard response is that a value like $6.3 million is not actually a price on an individual's life or death. Rather, it is a way of expressing the value of small risks of death. If people are willing to pay $6.30 to avoid a one in a million increase in the risk of death, then the "value of a statistical life" is $6.3 million.

It ignores the collective choice presented to society by most public health and environmental problems.

Under the cost-benefit approach, valuation of environmental benefits is based on individuals' private decisions as consumers or workers, not on their public values as citizens. However, policies that protect the environment are often public goods, and are not available for purchase in individual portions. In a classic example of this distinction, the philosopher Mark Sagoff found that his students, in their role as citizens, opposed commercial ski development in a nearby wilderness area, but, in their role as consumers, would plan to go skiing there if the development was built. There is no contradiction between these two views: as individual consumers, the students would have no way to express their collective preference for wilderness preservation. Their individual willingness to pay for skiing would send a misleading signal about their views as citizens.

It is often impossible to arrive at a meaningful social valuation by adding up the willingness to pay expressed by individuals. What could it mean to ask how much you personally are willing to pay to clean up a major oil spill? If no one else contributes, the clean-up won't happen regardless of your decision. As the Nobel Prize-winning economist Amartya Sen has pointed out, if your willingness to pay for a large-scale public initiative is independent of what others are paying, then you probably have

SHOULD WE LAUGH—OR CRY?

When it comes to cost-benefit analysis, nothing is out of bounds: everything has a price, and no inference is too heartless for the "hard science" of economics. The following stories are not the work of a lunatic fringe, but on the contrary, reflect how some of the most influential and well-known cost-benefit practitioners view the world.

Several years ago, states were suing tobacco companies for medical expenditures resulting from cigarette smoking. At that time, W. Kip Viscusi, a professor of law and economics at Harvard, concluded that states, in fact, *saved* money as the result of smoking by their citizens. Why? Because they died early, saving the states expenses on nursing home care and other services associated with an aging population! Viscusi even suggested that "cigarette smoking should be subsidized rather than taxed."

Take the problem of lead poisoning in children. One of the most serious and disturbing effects of lead is the neurological damage it can cause in young children, including permanently lowered mental ability. Randall Lutter, a researcher at the AEI-Brookings Joint Center for Regulatory Studies, put a dollar figure on the damage by looking at how much parents spent on a treatment designed to cause excretion of lead from the body. Parental spending on this treatment, according to Lutter, supports an estimate of $1,500 per IQ point lost due to lead poisoning. Previous economic analyses by EPA, based on the decrease in the children's expected future earnings, have estimated the value to be much higher—up to $9,000 per IQ point. Based on his lower figure, Lutter suggest that "agencies should consider relaxing their lead standards."

For sheer analytical audacity, Lutter's study faces some stiff competition from another study concerning children. Here, researchers examined mothers' car-seat fastening practices. They calculated the difference between the time required to fasten the seats correctly and the time mothers actually spent fastening their children into their seats. Then they assigned a monetary value to this interval of time based on the mothers' hourly wage rate (or, in the case of non-working moms, based on a guess at the wages they might have earned). When mothers saved time—and, by hypothesis, money—by fastening their children's car seats incorrectly, they were, according to the researchers, implicitly placing a finite monetary value on the life-threatening risks to their children posed by car accidents. Building on this calculation, the researchers were able to answer the vexing question of how much a statistical child's life is worth to her mother: $500,000.

not understood the nature of the problem.

It systematically downgrades the importance of the future.

One of the great triumphs of environmental law is that it seeks to avert harms to people and to natural resources in the future, and not only within this generation, but in future generations as well. Indeed, one of the primary objectives of the National

THE USE AND MISUSE OF COST-BENEFIT ANALYSIS: ARSENIC IN DRINKING WATER

One thing is certain: arsenic is bad for you. It causes cancers of the bladder, lungs, skin, kidneys, nasal passages, liver, and prostate, as well as other cardiovascular, pulmonary, neurological, immunological, and endocrine problems. It is found naturally in rock formations and dissolves into drinking water supplies, the principal source of exposure.

Starting in 1942, federal law set the standard limiting arsenic in drinking water to 50 parts per billion (ppb). In 1962, the U.S. Public Health Service recommended that drinking water should not contain more than 10 ppb. In January 2001, EPA finally adopted this standard (recommended by the World Health Organization and adopted by many European countries). Less than two months later, the Bush administration withdrew the new rule—only to accept it again after eight months of further review and debate.

In developing the new standard, EPA considered four possible standards: 3, 5, 10, and 20 ppb. On the cost side, detailed engineering descriptions are available for an array of possible technologies for water treatment and disposal of resulting residues. EPA's estimates express only a narrow range of uncertainty about costs. If the chosen pollution control technologies become cheaper once the arsenic rule is implemented—as often happens when environmental rules are enforced—the estimated costs will prove too high.

On the benefit side, reduction in arsenic in drinking water has many health advantages. However, EPA's analysts were only able to produce quantitative estimates of the health effects for bladder and lung cancer; all numerical analysis of benefits refers to preventing these two cancers alone. EPA set the value of an avoided death at $6.1 million in 1999 dollars, based on "wage-risk" studies measuring the wage premium required to attract workers to dangerous jobs. For other health effects, EPA found that there was no "willingness-to-pay" value available for nonfatal cancers—so it used the value of reducing chronic bronchitis instead! EPA did not provide a dollar equivalent at all for health effects other than bladder and lung cancers.

The range between the upper and lower estimates of health benefits reflects solely the uncertainty about the number of avoided cancers. Costs and monetized benefits are roughly comparable for 20 ppb and 10 ppb. At 5 ppb and 3 ppb, the monetized benefits are below the costs.

AEI-BROOKINGS ANALYSIS

The AEI-Brookings Joint Center for Regulatory Studies has been a vocal proponent of cost-benefit analysis of environmental rules. Nevertheless, when EPA first issued its new arsenic rule, AEI-Brookings produced a highly critical study authored by Robert Hahn and Jason Burnett. EPA had erred in two ways, the AEI-Brookings study concluded, which led to overestimates of the benefits of arsenic reduction.

Environmental Policy Act, which has been called our basic charter of environmental protection, is to nudge the nation into "fulfill[ing] the responsibilities of each generation as trustee of the environment for succeeding generations."

The time periods involved in protecting the environment are often enormous—even many centuries, in such cases as climate change, radioactive waste, etc. With time spans this long, any discounting will make even global catastrophes seem trivial.

First, the study criticized EPA for failing to discount the lives saved by the arsenic rule. Because exposure to arsenic leads to cancer only after a latency period, Hahn and Burnett thought EPA should have discounted the benefits of the rule. Without citing any arsenic-related scientific evidence, Hahn and Burnett picked a latency period of 30 years as their "best estimate." This guess, combined with a 7 percent discount rate, had the effect of reducing the present value of a life saved from $6.1 million to $1.1 million.

Second, the AEI-Brookings study criticized EPA for assuming that the number of cancer cases due to arsenic is proportional to total exposure. Making up a different relationship between exposure and cancer, Hahn and Burnett, neither of whom is a scientist, guessed that there were only one-fifth as many cases of cancer due to arsenic as EPA had projected. With these and other adjustments, Hahn and Burnett found the costs of arsenic reduction to be roughly ten times the benefits, costing a shocking $65 million per life saved. They speculated that even 50 ppb might be too strict a standard, in light of the low benefits.

When the National Academy of Sciences (NAS) reviewed the arsenic standard yet again, in 2001, it found exactly the opposite of Hahn and Burnett's "best estimate." That is, NAS concluded that arsenic would cause more cancer cases than EPA had projected. This finding, no doubt combined with the public outcry over the issue, helped persuade the Bush administration to relent and accept the 10 ppb standard.

PUBLIC DEBATE

Once the rival EPA and Hahn-Burnett numbers made their way into the public forum, the assumptions, qualifications, and uncertainties surrounding them were forgotten.

The *Washington Post*, for example, ran a series of opinion pieces criticizing EPA's 10 ppb standard when originally issued in early 2001. Because the rule was predicted to cost $210 billion and the benefits were valued at $170 billion, these essays concluded that the rule was not worth it. They completely ignored the many unquantified benefits EPA had felt certain would flow from the rule.

The articles also referred to the Hahn-Burnett analysis without even mentioning the discounting and the dubious estimates that so influenced its results. Journalist Michael Kinsley noted the $65 million price tag per life saved according to Hahn and Burnett's analysis, and opined, without dwelling on the details, that its assumptions seemed "reasonable."

The public dialogue in the aftermath of the Bush administration's initial withdrawal of the new arsenic rule was not about discounting future life-saving, or cancer risk assessment, or the value of a life. Yet the numerical estimates of the benefits turn almost entirely on these issues, and the theories on which they rest. Cost-benefit analysis has not enriched the public dialogue; it has impoverished it, covering the topic with poorly understood numbers rather than clarifying the underlying clash of values.

At a discount rate of 5%, for example, the deaths of a billion people 500 years from now becomes less serious than the death of one person today. Seen in this way, discounting looks like a fancy justification for foisting our problems off onto the people who come after us.

It ignores considerations of distribution and fairness.

Cost-benefit analysis adds up all the costs of a policy, adds up all the benefits, and compares the totals. Implicit in this innocuous-sounding procedure is the assumption that it doesn't matter who gets the benefits and who pays the costs. Yet isn't there is an important difference between spending state tax revenues, say, to improve the parks in rich communities, and spending the same revenues to clean up pollution in poor communities?

The problem of equity runs even deeper. Benefits are typically measured by willingness to pay for environmental improvement, and the rich are able and willing to pay for more than the poor. Imagine a cost-benefit analysis of locating an undesirable facility, such as a landfill or incinerator. Wealthy communities are willing to pay more for the benefit of not having the facility in their backyards; thus, under the logic of cost-benefit analysis, the net benefits to society will be maximized by putting the facility in a low-income area. In reality, pollution is typically dumped on the poor without waiting for formal analysis. Still, cost-benefit analysis rationalizes and reinforces the problem, allowing environmental burdens to flow downhill along the income slopes of an unequal society.

Conclusion

There is nothing objective about the basic premises of cost-benefit analysis. Treating individuals solely as consumers, rather than as citizens with a sense of moral responsibility, represents a distinct and highly questionable worldview. Likewise, discounting reflects judgments about the nature of environmental risks and citizens' responsibilities toward future generations.

These assumptions beg fundamental questions about ethics and equity, and one cannot decide whether to embrace them without thinking through the whole range of moral issues they raise. Yet once one has thought through these issues, there is no need then to collapse the complex moral inquiry into a series of numbers. Pricing the priceless just translates our inquiry into a different language, one with a painfully impoverished vocabulary.

This article is a condensed version of the report *Pricing the Priceless*, published by the Georgetown Environmental Law and Policy Institute at Georgetown University Law Center. The full report *Pricing the Priceless* is available on-line at <www.ase.tufts.edu/gdae/publications/C-B% 20pamphlet%20final.pdf>. Ackerman and Heinzerling's book on these and related issues, Priceless: Human Health, the Environment, and the Limits of the Market, will be published by The New Press in January 2004.

LET'S JUST ASSUME WE'RE SUSTAINABLE

WILLIAM E. REES

May/June 1997

"If it is very easy to substitute other factors for natural resources, then ... the world can, in effect, get along without natural resources, so exhaustion is just an event not a catastrophe." So wrote Nobel-winning economist Robert Solow in 1974. If we don't think about it much, this statement seems innocuous enough. The internal logic is impeccable and very comforting to those nervous about the state of the world. Probe a little deeper, however, and we find that Solow's message lies at the heart of a major controversy among economists concerning whether the economy—and society—are sustainable despite increasingly depleted and polluted resources in the long run.

Those on Solow's side believe that technology can substitute for nature. If we run out of some resource, human ingenuity and inventiveness will rally to find a replacement. Most economists in wealthy countries generally accept this argument.

But their ecologically minded colleagues question Solow's assumption that it is "very easy" to find substitutes for natural resources and processes. The ozone layer, for instance, may not be easily replaceable. If not, then our present economy is not organized in an "environmentally sustainable" way.

The controversy is tied to recent advances in capital theory. In the past decade, economists have begun to recognize that resources are a unique type of capital capable of producing income indefinitely into the future. For example, every year properly managed fish stocks can produce a catch that can be sustained into the future; if left intact, stratospheric ozone delivers continuous protection against harmful ultraviolet radiation. So-called "natural capital" has thus gained the same weight and theoretical status as the more familiar human-made capital—factories, machinery, and equipment.

This expanded concept of capital is now being used by both sides in the debate to develop measures of sustainability. From the perspective of capital theory, no economy is sustainable if it depletes productive assets, whether natural or human-made. An economy is only sustainable if it passes on the same per capita stock of capital from one generation to the next. But while this basic principle has gained wide acceptance in recent years, controversy remains over the degree to which manufactured capital can substitute for natural capital.

Neoclassical economists and other analysts generally assume that the two forms of capital are interchangeable. By this interpretation, depleting natural resources—natural capital—does not matter so long as part of the money generated by resource use is invested in manufactured capital of equivalent value. Because the neoclassical view makes no distinction between natural and human-made assets, this variation on the theme is referred to as "weak sustainability."

To many non-economists, it is a long stretch to assume that natural and human-made capital can just substitute for one another. However, the argument is not entirely groundless. Economists assume (yes, another assumption) that you can measure the scarcity of a good by its market price. Repeated studies since the 1960s have shown that the real prices of most resources bought and sold on the market have remained stable or have actually fallen over the past century. Economists take this as evidence that any hint of scarcity for a natural commodity stimulates human ingenuity to find a substitute, thus conserving the original resource. Sometimes the substitution is the functional equivalent, as when metal studs replace wooden ones in construction. As often, however, we invent an entirely new technology with different or educed material requirements. Think of how much copper wire has been saved by the development of microwave communication, the adoption of printed circuit boards, and the invention of optical fibers. (These fibers are as thin as a human hair and can carry more information more accurately than a thick bundle of copper wires.)

Examples like this are sometimes used to press the substitution argument to extremes. For instance, because optical fiber is itself not found in nature but is made from silicon (the second-most abundant element in the Earth's crust), technological optimists proclaim that resources are actually more the product of the human mind than of nature. Thus, in 1990, Walter Block, then senior economist at the Fraser Institute (a Canadian neoconservative think tank), argued the benefits of continuous population growth on the grounds that "additional people can create more resources than they use up, thanks to technological improvements..." More recently, the University of Maryland's famed growth advocate, Julian Simon, wrote: "Technology exists now to produce in virtually inexhaustible quantities just about all the products made by nature..."

Extremes aside, most economists and planners today do favor the "weak sustainability" model. Indeed, it undergirds their model of international development driven by continuous material growth, globalization, liberalized trade—and the depletion of natural capital.

Ecological economists, on the other hand, are less sanguine about human prospects than their mainstream colleagues. They observe that natural and manufactured capital often complement each other in the production process and cannot always substitute for one another. For example, more fishing boats are no substitute for a depleted stock of fish. In fact, since human-made capital is made from natural capital and requires natural resources to function, then natural capital is a prerequisite for manufactured capital.

In any event, it is becoming clear that certain crucial goods and services of nature are essential to human life and the economy. They cannot be substituted, and if lost, they are lost forever. Exhausting the stock of certain types of natural capital could therefore be catastrophic (as may be the case with stratospheric ozone, currently being depleted by CFCs and other industrial chemicals made from chlorine and bromine). It seems, therefore, that Solow's assumption is false, and if so, both the notion of weak sustainability and the prevailing model of global development collapse.

Ecologically minded analysts therefore support a "strong sustainability" argument instead. This is a more cautious model in which renewable natural capital and manufactured capital must each be maintained intact for the next generation. Strong sustainability implies that humankind must learn to live on the annual income of goods and "life support services" of air, water and the like, generated by the natural capital stocks we have left. If the population grows, so should our natural capital stocks.

There are other reasons to be suspicious of the weak sustainability model. Economists measure the natural capital stock using customary accounting methods, including market prices. But markets only work well with familiar, easily quantified material and energy commodities. The assimilation of wastes, "life support," aesthetic and spiritual values—all important services provided by the environment—are difficult to price or are simply invisible to conventional analysis. These may be lost forever as the stocks that produce them are liquidated or converted to human-made capital. For example, as forests are clear-cut for lumber and wood fiber, we lose their carbon sink functions—a key to the stability of the globe's climate—their water regulation and flood control services, and their biodiversity and spiritual values. How can we have confidence in a view of sustainability that does not account for such enormous wealth simply because it cannot be priced in the marketplace?

If the prevailing system of costs, prices and incentives fails absolutely as an indicator of impending scarcity, it is no surprise that conventional economic analyses raise few concerns about potential unsustainability. Instead, those who sound the ecological alarm are usually biologists and others who work with physical data on the state of the world.

One final problem. It turns out that many countries cannot meet standards for even weak sustainability. Worse, many that do, such as Germany, the Netherlands, Japan, and the United States, survive only by appropriating the ecological output of a land and sea area vastly larger than their own domestic territories. While they may seem economically sustainable, these high-income economies are running massive "ecological deficits" with the rest of the world. They draw on the Third World for resources, locate high-polluting industries and landfills there, and generally abuse the global commons. Thus, their high-flying lifestyles cannot be extended sustainably to all of humanity using prevailing technology.

No wonder the international community is having such difficulty defining a criterion for sustainability that is ecologically rigorous. Accepting strong sustainability would require significant government intervention in the economy and a radical transformation of consumer values and behavior. Weak sustainability is certainly easier to swallow—it virtually assumes we are already sustainable.

Resources: Steady State Economics, Herman Daly (Island Press, 1991); "Capital Theory and the Measurement of Sustainable Development: An Indicator of Weak Sustainability," David W. Pearce and Giles D. Atkinson, *Ecological Economics* 8, 1993; "Ecological Footprints and Appropriated Carrying Capacity: Measuring the Natural Capital Requirements of the Human Economy," William Rees and M. Wackernagel, in A.M. Jansson et al., *Investing in Natural Capital: The Ecological Economics Approach to Sustainability* (Island Press, 1994); "How Strong Is Weak Sustainability?" P. Victor et al., *Economie Applique* XLVIII, 1995; "The Economics of Resources or the Resources of Economics," Robert Solow, *American Economics Review* 2, 1974; "The State of Humanity: Steadily Improving," Julian Simon, The Cato Institute, 1995.

CHAPTER 2

CORPORATE POWER AND ENVIRONMENTAL POLICY

INDUSTRY ATTACKS ON DISSENT

FROM RACHEL CARSON TO OPRAH

Forty years after the publication of Silent Spring, corporations are still "producing poisons—and still trying to keep critics from fighting back.

LAURA ORLANDO

March/April 2002

In March 1996, the British government announced that ten people had died after eating beef from cattle sick with "mad cow disease." A month later, financier, movie actress, and talk-show host Oprah Winfrey discussed the topic on national television. While interviewing guest Howard Lyman of the Humane Society about his belief that American cattle might be at risk for the disease, Winfrey told her audience, "It has just stopped me cold from eating another burger." A group of Texas cattle ranchers sued Winfrey and Lyman for libeling cattle. Four years and over $1 million later, the two were vindicated in court.

Winfrey and Lyman were sued under the Texas False Disparagement of Perishable Food Products Act. Food disparagement laws are a new tool in an old bag of tricks used by corporations to protect their own economic interests at the expense of public discussion. Silencing public debate with frivolous, time-consuming, and costly lawsuits has become so commonplace that the technique has its own name: strategic lawsuits against public participation, or SLAPP suits.

Winfrey and Lyman won in lower federal court because the judge ruled that cattle were not "perishable food products." The cattlemen pursued the matter in appellate court. A three-judge panel eventually ruled against the Texas ranchers. But the SLAPP suit achieved its objective by forcing Winfrey and Lyman to spend an enormous amount of time and money defending themselves—and by serving as a warning to the rest of us that saying what we believe to be true may cost us more than we can bear.

Lawsuits, and the threat of lawsuits, are not the only means industry uses to stifle dissent. Industry routinely buys the science that suits its needs (tobacco is a good example) and according to Sheldon Rampton, editor of the newsletter *PR Watch*, spends at least $10 billion every year on "public relations."

Industry's use of half-truths and intimidation to defend its toxic assault on life is nothing new. But until 40 years ago, when Rachel Carson's book *Silent Spring* was published, one could argue that we—the people—didn't know what was going on. *Silent Spring* woke up the nation, creating a national consciousness about the health and environmental consequences of pesticide use. Industry woke up too. Bruce Johnson, a Seattle lawyer, told the *New York Times* in 1999, "If [food disparagement laws] had been in place in the 1960s, Rachel Carson might not have found a publisher willing to print *Silent Spring*."

Trying to Silence *Silent Spring*

Before World War I, about half of the industrial products in the United States were made from renewable resources, such as plant-, wood-, and animal-based materials. In the 1920s and 1930s, oil and chemical companies like Union Carbide, Shell, and Dow expanded their interest in petrochemical manufacturing. The petrochemical industry, strengthened immensely by World War II, replaced renewable materials with synthetic organic compounds made from the by-products of oil and natural gas: for instance, synthetic rubber replaced natural rubber, chemical detergents replaced animal-based soaps, and polyester replaced cotton. In the 1950s and 1960s, the thriving plastics industry accelerated the shift even more. Today, 92% of the materials used for U.S. products and production processes are nonrenewable.

In many cases, the processes used to manufacture synthetic products created toxic wastes, and often the products themselves—either intact or when dissipated into the environment—were harmful to life. Among the most lethal of these products were synthetic pesticides. Before 1940, most pesticides were made from plants; a few were made from toxic metals like arsenic and mercury. But the synthetic chemicals created for chemical warfare during World War II were found to be highly effective weed and insect killers. So in 1945, with strong government backing, these poisons entered commercial markets. Within ten years, synthetic pesticides had captured 90% of the agricultural pest-control market. Pesticides such as dichloro diphenyl trichloroethane (DDT), dieldrin, and aldrin were dropped from planes like bombs over Dresden.

State and federal government agencies blanketed neighborhoods with poisons in an attempt to eradicate pests like gypsy moths and Japanese beetles. Farmers used DDT and other synthetic insecticides on a variety of crops, including cotton, peanuts, and soybeans. Suburbanites embraced the new chemicals in their war against perceived nuisances like crab grass and dandelions.

Few people understood the dangers to life that these new chemicals presented. Sickness and death among chemical manufacturing workers were sometimes the first indication that the materials they worked with were toxic. But most people believed that you had to be an industrial worker to get sick. Rachel Carson's *Silent Spring* was the first widely read publication to say that everybody was being poisoned.

Silent Spring was serialized by *The New Yorker* in June 1962 and came out in book form that same year. The book was—and still is—a devastating testament to the mortal dangers of synthetic chemical poisons. Carson, a wildlife biologist with two best sellers and a National Book Award under her belt, wrote, "We allow the chemical death rain to fall as though there were no alternative, whereas in fact there are many, and our ingenuity could soon discover many more if given opportunity."

Silent Spring was written before big business politics and sophistry were so well versed at setting the terms of discourse about environmental issues. Still, during the four years that Carson spent writing the book, she was well aware that it would unleash the wrath of the chemical industry. Deeply concerned about potential industry attacks and lawsuits, she did what she could to protect herself. Carson and her literary agent Marie Rodell asked lawyers from Houghton Mifflin, her publisher, to review the manuscript. Carson made sure Houghton Mifflin had libel insurance and she renegotiated a contract with them that put a monetary limit on her personal liability. And building the best defense of all, she meticulously checked her facts and diligently worked on a list of principal sources to document her conclusions.

Carson's concerns were well founded. After *The New Yorker* serialized parts of the book, the *New York Times* ran an article with the headline, " '*Silent Spring*' Is Now Noisy Summer: Pesticide Industry Up In Arms Over a New Book." The story began, "The $300,000,000 pesticides industry has been highly irritated by a quiet woman author whose previous works on science have been praised for the beauty and precision of the writing." It quoted the president of the Montrose Chemical Corporation—a major manufacturer of DDT, a pesticide that Carson discussed at length—as saying that Carson wrote not "as a scientist but rather as a fanatic defender of the cult of the balance of nature."

Some of the criticism seems laughable now. After the second installment from *Silent Spring* appeared in *The New Yorker*, a man from California wrote to the magazine:

> Miss Rachel Carson's reference to the selfishness of insecticide manufacturers probably reflects her Communist sympathies, like a lot of our writers these days. We can live without birds and animals, but, as the current market slump shows, we cannot live without business. As for insects, isn't it just like a woman to be scared to

> death of a few little bugs! As long as we have the H-bomb everything will be O.K.
> P.S. She's probably a peace-nut too.

But industry's attack on Rachel Carson was swift and vicious. The chemical companies banded together and hired a public relations firm to malign the book and attack Carson's credibility. The pesticide industry trade group, the National Agricultural Chemicals Association, spent over $250,000 (equivalent to $1.4 million today) to denigrate the book and its author. The company that manufactured and sold the pesticides chlordane and heptachlor, the Velsicol Chemical Company of Chicago, threatened to sue Houghton Mifflin.

Milton Greenstein, legal counsel and vice president of *The New Yorker*, was called by at least one chemical company and told that the magazine would be sued if it didn't pull the last installment it planned to run of Carson's book. Greenstein responded, "Everything in those articles has been checked and is true. Go ahead and sue." John Vosburgh, editor of Audubon Magazine, which published excerpts from *Silent Spring*, said pretty much the same thing when Audubon was threatened. According to Carson biographer Linda Lear, Velsicol's lawyers suggested to Vosburgh that printing "a muckraking article containing unwarranted assertions about Velsicol pesticides" might "jeopardize [the] financial security" of magazine employees and their families. Vosburgh was so incensed that he wrote an editorial that appeared with the book excerpts, criticizing the chemical industry's response.

Industry threats did not stop the publication of *Silent Spring*, nor did the attacks prevent the book from becoming wildly successful. Carson was a popular writer who had the support of her editors, her publisher, and even President Kennedy, who cited *Silent Spring* as a reason to examine the health effects of pesticides. After the book was published, Carson was interviewed by Eric Severeid on national television and she testified before Congress about chemical poisons. She was profiled in Life magazine and featured in the *New York Times* and the *Washington Post*. In a review for the Book-of-the-Month Club, Supreme Court Justice William O. Douglas wrote that *Silent Spring* "is a call for immediate action and for effective control of all merchants of poison," and called the book "the most important chronicle of this century for the human race."

Carson effectively got her message across in part because what she had to say was radically new to the public, because her facts were unassailable, and because industry, though quite capable of attacking her and the publications that featured her work, had not yet learned how to overload the media—and by extension the people—with its own point of view.

Today's Targets

Rachel Carson understood the forces at work in government and industry. Having served on the staff of the U.S. Fish and Wildlife Service for 16 years, she was well aware of government's role in promoting and defending chemical poisons. "The crusade to create a chemically sterile, insect-free world," Carson wrote, "seems to have engendered a fanatic zeal on the part of many specialists and most of the so-called control agencies." We were living, she said, in an era "dominated by industry, in which the right to make a dollar at whatever cost is seldom challenged. When the public protests, confronted with some obvious evidence of damaging results of pesticide applications, it is fed little tranquilizing pills of half truth. We urgently need an end to these false assurances, to the sugar coating of unpalatable facts."

This language is too mild to describe what is happening today. Not only has the production of chemical poisons continued, but the chemical industry has become much more skillful at manipulating the media for its own ends. Now we are fed big pills of outright lies, prevarication, and deception. We do not need to see industry's press releases; we hear the corporate viewpoint every day, all the time. Forty years after Rachel Carson tripped the alarm bell, we have been largely conditioned by industry to accept that which is harmful to us and to reject the warning signs of environmental devastation. We have been made ready to believe that a conservation ethic is incompatible with prosperity and that with creature comforts come sacrifices. Many of us want the sugar coating because, to a great extent, we are consumer junkies who believe that, if we demand that industry change its behavior, we will have to change our own.

But of course not everyone wants the sugar coating, and some people are writing and talking about environmental issues in ways that are as compelling as *Silent Spring*. It is just harder to hear them now, harder to unpeel the layers of deception created by corporations and regulators. And when dissenting voices are heard, industry is quick to strike back.

For example, two recent books, *Living Downstream* and *Our Stolen Future*, are filled with the kind of critical thinking and meticulous research found in Carson's *Silent Spring*. Both deal with the chemical causes and consequences of health and environmental degradation. Both take industry to task. Both were attacked.

Sandra Steingraber's 1997 book, *Living Downstream: An Ecologist Looks at Cancer and the Environment*, is the *Silent Spring* of the post-baby boom generation. Viewing cancer through several lenses—as biologist, cancer survivor, poet, and activist—Steingraber shows the links between cancer and environmental degradation. The book is beautifully written and powerfully frank. Reviewer Nancy Evans wrote: "The author describes the many kinds of silence that surround cancer issues, personal and political, individual and collective. The silence of scientists who fear loss of funding, the silence that fear imposes on people with cancer and those at risk. She suggests that *Silent Spring* shows us 'how one kind of silence breeds another, how the secrecies of government beget a weirdly quiet and lifeless world.' "

Living Downstream was also reviewed in the New England Journal of Medicine in November 1998. The negative review was signed "Jerry H. Berke, M.D., M.P.H." Trouble is, the journal failed to note Berke's affiliation with the W.R. Grace Company, a notorious environmental polluter.

Berke, director of toxicology for W.R. Grace, began his review with an attack on all environmentalists: "An older colleague of mine once suggested that the work product of an environmentalist is controversy. Fear and the threat of unseen, unchosen hazards enhance fund-raising for environmental political organizations and fund environmental research, he suggested." Berke called Steingraber's book "biased" and "obsessed with environmental pollution." And like a loyal industry toxicologist, he wrote, "The focus on environmental pollution and agricultural chemicals to explain human cancer has simply not been fruitful nor given rise to useful preventive strategies."

The mainstream media essentially ignored *Living Downstream*. No one can say exactly why, but one can guess that the book didn't win any points in the corporate-controlled media by eloquently pressing for prevention and suggesting that people change the way they think about chemicals. The book calls for a "human rights approach," which would recognize that the "current system of regulating the use, release, and disposal of known and suspected carcinogens—rather than preventing their generation in the first place—is intolerable."

Like *Living Downstream*, *Our Stolen Future*—a book about endocrine disrupters (synthetic chemicals that disrupt hormones)—has also come under fire. When it was published in 1996, *Our Stolen Future* caused an immediate stir. Using a new way to examine the effects of chemical contamination, authors Theo Colborn, Dianne Dumanoski, and John Peterson Myers provide evidence that endocrine disruptors are widespread in the environment and are making people sick. A staggering list of synthetic chemicals, they tell us, interferes with hormones in humans and wildlife. These chemicals are common in the manufacture of pesticides, herbicides, and petrochemicals: they are found in soaps and detergents, flame retardants, and the dioxins produced in pulp and paper mills. In humans, the presence of endocrine disruptors can result in, among other things, severe reproductive tract deformities, declines in sperm count, elevated risk of cancer, and even behavioral changes. *Our Stolen Future* makes a powerful case for caution when using these chemicals.

But industry was having none of it. As Sheldon Rampton and John Stauber point out in Trust Us, We're Experts!, industry's attack on the book was "instant and vicious." The industry-funded Advancement of Sound Science Coalition held a press conference at which no fewer than ten scientists labeled the book as "fiction." And another industry-financed group, the American Council on Science and Health, "obtained a copy of the book in galley form months before publication and prepared an 11-page attack on it before it even hit the bookstores." Not surprisingly, the Wall Street Journal referred to *Our Stolen Future* as an "environmental 'hype machine.' "

One chemical industry leader, the Monsanto Company, has a long record of going after its critics. Monsanto manufactured DDT and polychlorinated biphenyls (PCBs) before they were banned by the U.S. Environmental Protection Agency in the 1970s. It still makes a long list of synthetic chemicals and aggressively markets genetically engineered products like bovine growth hormone (Posilac) and genetically modified seeds. A billion-dollar company when *Silent Spring* first appeared, it published a parody of Carson's work, called "The Desolate Year," in the October 1962 issue of *Monsanto Magazine*. Since then, Monsanto has become a corporate role model in sugar-coating unpalatable facts and silencing dissent.

For example, *Against the Grain: Biotechnology and the Corporate Takeover of Your Food*, a book by Dr. Marc Lappé and Britt Bailey, was originally supposed to be published by Vital Health. But the company cancelled publication after receiving a threatening letter from a Monsanto lawyer, who said he believed the manuscript contained false statements about Monsanto's biggest money maker, the herbicide RoundUp. Common Courage Press picked up the book and published it in 1998.

That same year, *The Ecologist* magazine published a special issue, "The Monsanto Files," which took a critical look at the chemical/biotechnology giant. But *The Ecologist*'s printer, Penwells of Saltash Cornwall (with whom *The Ecologist* had worked for 29 years), destroyed the 14,000 copy print run without even notifying the magazine. Penwells refused to comment on its decision and Monsanto denied any responsibility for the action, prompting *The Ecologist*'s editor, Zac Goldsmith, to say, "The fact that Monsanto had nothing to do with the decision to pulp is, if anything, more scary than if they had made some kind of legal threat. It goes to show what a powerful force a reputation can be." The magazine was able to line up another printer for the Monsanto issue.

In both cases, Monsanto's critics managed to find other venues for getting their information out to the public. But, like the SLAPP suit waged against Oprah Winfrey and Howard Lyman, the chemical company's actions—or maybe only its reputation for doing damage—caused serious disruption along the way. It's all part of a sophisticated set of techniques that industry uses to take the legs out from under dissent.

PROJECTED GROWTH IN CHEMICALS PRODUCTION ($), WORLD GROSS DOMESTIC PRODUCT (GDP), AND WORLD POPULATION

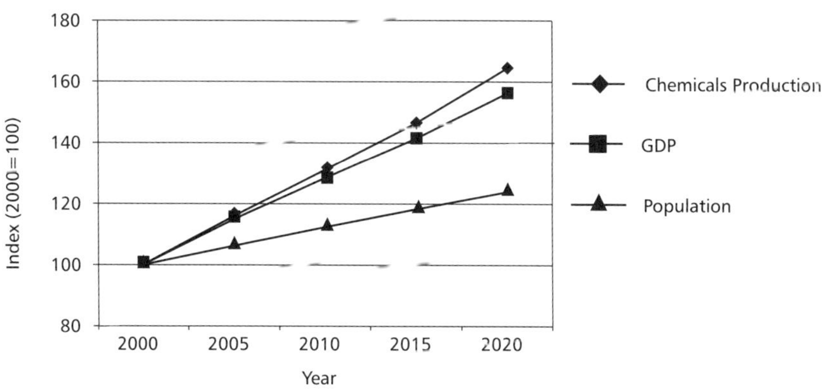

Source: Organization for Economic Cooperation and Development

The Obligation to Act

Forty years ago, Rachel Carson wrote, "We have fallen into a mesmerized state that makes us accept as inevitable that which is inferior or detrimental, as though having lost the will or the vision to demand that which is good?" (Perhaps the question mark expresses Carson's wish to be hopeful.) Today, we are up against an immensely more organized, coordinated, and powerful corporate PR machine than Carson or the early environmentalists faced. Although some people have woken up, it is hard not to feel numb when faced with yet another story about environmental degradation and chemical poisoning.

The facts about chemical production today are sobering. The world uses five billion pounds of pesticides every year, with almost half used in the United States. According to the Federal Emergency Management Agency, as many as 500,000 U.S. products pose physical or health hazards and can be defined as "hazardous chemicals." U.S. industry uses 70,000 different chemical substances, but there is little or no attempt to assess their health or environmental impacts. Each year, over 1,000 new synthetic chemicals are introduced in the United States. But only a small fraction of these are tested for carcinogenity or endocrine disruption, and there is little understanding of how they interact with each other. The list of known poisons is long and troubling. It is as if we have forgotten, or have never known, "that which is good."

It is hard to be hopeful. In a chapter entitled "To the Ends of the Earth," *Our Stolen Future* follows a PCB molecule from its creation in a Monsanto chemical plant near Anniston, Alabama, to its entry into a polar bear in the Arctic. That chemical has now made its way to court, in the blood of thousands of Anniston residents who are suing Monsanto for knowingly dumping PCBs in their community. In January 2002, during opening arguments, a Monsanto lawyer carried on the company's long tradition of denial and deceit: "We would all rather live in a pristine world. We are all going to be exposed to things on a daily basis. Our bodies can deal with it."

We can't address the environmental crisis without going right to industry's door. A good first step is to hold industries accountable for the pollution they generate and the harm they cause. In places like Anniston, people are trying. But the greatest impact will come from fundamentally changing what corporations produce and how. This could be done by making laws based on, for example, the Precautionary Principle, which says that if there is reasonable suspicion that a technology, process, or chemical could be harmful, its application should be altered or it should be stopped altogether—even if some cause-and-effect relationships have not been fully established scientifically. Moreover, the burden of proof lies with the activity's proponents and not with the general public. This is not a "fringe" idea. The European Commission (the executive body of the European Union responsible for implementing and managing policy) and some nations, such as Sweden and Germany, have adopted the Precautionary Principle as part of a structured approach to risk analysis. In 1997, the state of Massachusetts enacted a law that uses the Precautionary Principle as a guide for preventing toxic pollution.

Carson wrote, "The obligation to endure gives us the right to know." We know much more now than we did 40 years ago. If we are to endure, then we are also obligated to act. Human ingenuity has in it immense resources for good: by making good choices, we can live well without destroying life.

Resources: Rachel Carson, *Silent Spring* (Houghton Mifflin, 1962); Theo Colborn, Dianne Dumanoski, and John Peterson Myers, *Our Stolen Future* (Dutton, 1996) <www.ourstolenfuture.com>; Linda Lear, Rachel Carson: *Witness for Nature* (Henry Holt, 1997); Sheldon Rampton and John Stauber, *Trust Us, We're Experts! How Industry Manipulates Science and Gambles with Your Future* (Jeremy P. Tarcher/Putnam, 2001) <www.prwatch.org>; Sandra Steingraber, *Living Downstream: An Ecologist Looks at Cancer and the Environment* (Addison-Wesley, 1997) <www.steingraber.com>.

WAR ON THE EARTH

BOB FELDMAN

March/April 2003

In this era of "permanent war," the U.S. war machine bombards civilians in places like Serbia, Afghanistan, and Iraq. It also makes "war on the earth," both at home and abroad. The U.S. Department of Defense is, in fact, the world's largest polluter, producing more hazardous waste per year than the five largest U.S. chemical companies combined. Washington's Fairchild Air Force Base, the number one producer of hazardous waste among domestic military bases, generated over 13 million pounds of waste in 1997 (more than the weight of the Eiffel Tower's iron structure). Oklahoma's Tinker Air Force Base, the top toxic waste emitter, released over 600,000 pounds in the same year (the same amount of water would cover an entire football field about two inches deep).

Just about every U.S. military base and nuclear arms facility emits toxics into the environment. At many U.S. military target ranges, petroleum products and heavy metals used in bombs and bullets contaminate the soil and groundwater. And since the Pentagon operates its bases as "federal reservations," they are usually beyond the reach of local and state environmental regulations. Local and state authorities often do not find out the extent of the toxic contamination until after a base is closed down.

Active and abandoned military bases have released toxic pollution from Cape Cod to San Diego, Alaska to Hawaii. In June 2001, the Military Toxics Project and the Environmental Health Coalition released the report "Defend Our Health: A People's Report to Congress," detailing the Pentagon's "war on the earth" in the United States and Puerto Rico. (See map on p. 35.) The contaminants emitted from military bases include pesticides, solvents, petroleum, lead, mercury, and uranium. The health effects for the surrounding communities are devastating: miscarriages, low birth weights, birth defects, kidney disease, and cancer.

Even the Defense Department itself now acknowledges some of the environmental destruction wrought by the U.S. military worldwide. The Pentagon's own

Inspector General documented, in a 1999 report, pollution at U.S. bases in Canada, Germany, Great Britain, Greenland, Iceland, Italy, Panama, the Philippines, South Korea, Spain, and Turkey. Again, since even U.S. military bases abroad are treated as U.S. territory, the installations typically remain exempt from the environmental authority of the host country.

Activists worldwide have called attention to the scourge of toxic pollution, target-range bombardment, noise pollution, abandoned munitions, and radioactive waste unleashed by U.S. bases. (See map on pp. 35, 37, and 38.) The International Grassroots Summit on Military Bases Cleanup in 1999 brought together 70 representatives of citizen groups affected by U.S. military contamination. The gathering adopted an "Environmental Bill of Rights for Persons, Indigenous Peoples, Communities and Nations Hosting Foreign and Colonial Military Bases," declaring that past and present military bases "threaten health, welfare, and the environment, [as well as] future generations." The document emphasizes that the burden of environmental destruction has fallen disproportionately on "economically disadvantaged communities, women, children, people of color and indigenous people." And it demands that the "foreign and colonial" armed forces responsible for the contamination bear the costs the cleanup."

Yet until the era of "permanent war" and global U.S. militarism gives way to an era of world peace, the U.S. military machine will likely remain above the law. And the Pentagon will continue its "war on the earth."

Resources: Safety Forum Research/Safetyforum. com <www.safetyforum.com>; Military Toxics Project and Environmental Health Coalition, "Defend Our Health: A People's Report to Congress," (June 2001); Greenpeace <www.greenpeace.org>; East Asia/U.S. Women's Network Against Militarism <www.apcjp.org/womens_network/skorea.htm>; Okinawan Peace Network of Los Angeles <www. uchinanchu.org>; Organization for the Prohibition of Chemical Weapons Technical Assistance Visit, Final Report, 8/14/01; *Financial Times*, 9/7/01; Ecocompass/IslandPress; Fellowship of Reconciliation Panama Campaign <www. forusa.org/program/panama>; Coastal Post newsmonthly <www.coastalpost.com>

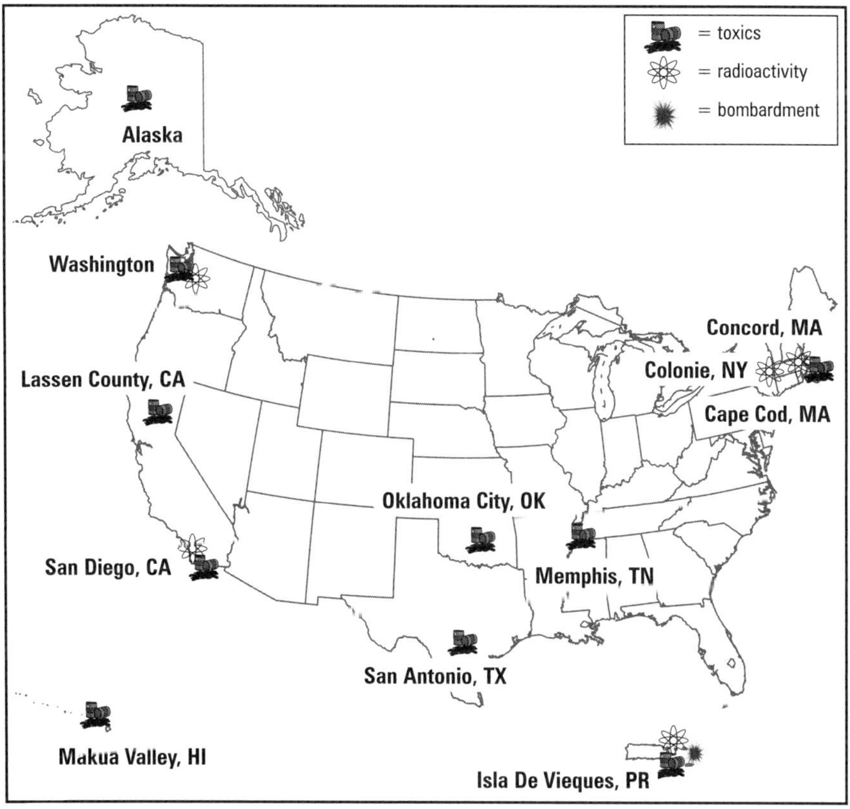

MAKUA VALLEY, HI: In the Makua Valley, the U.S. Army's live-fire assault training has caused fires and erosion and introduced alien plants and animals. These activities have threatened over 40 endangered plant and animal species, including the elpano bird. Homes and churches have also been destroyed by the fires and erosion. In addition, heavy metals and other pollutants from the base have contaminated the soil and groundwater.

ALASKA: U.S. military land fills, drum storage areas, fuel spill areas, and leaking underground storage tanks have polluted communities surrounding Cape Romanzof Long Range Radar station in Hooper Bay, Alaska. While fishing near Fort Greeley, Alaska, members of local indigenous tribes have found canisters of mustard gas left over from the 1950s and 1960s—when the U.S. military tested biological and chemical weapons at the site.

WASHINGTON: The U.S. Navy is the leading cause of oil spills off the Washington coast. The Navy spilled over 10,000 gallons of oil into Puget Sound in 1998. It also tests depleted uranium weapons in prime fishing waters nearby.

LASSEN COUNTY, CA: The Sierra Army Depot—where the military burns and detonates munitions—ranked as California's top source of air pollution in 1999, releasing 17% of all the toxic air emissions for the entire state. Increased cancer rates have been reported in both the surrounding county and the nearby Pyramid Lake Indian Reservation in Nevada.

SAN DIEGO, CA: The largest polluter in San Diego is the U.S. Navy, which has created 100 toxic and radioactive waste sites in San Diego Bay over the last eighty years. The National Oceanic and Atmospheric Administration found that the bay had the country's second-most-toxic estuary sediments, with the pollution concentrated around Navy and Navy-contractor sites. Fish in San Diego Bay contain high levels of mercury and radioactive compounds. The Navy also spilled over 11,000 gallons of oil into the bay in 1998.

OKLAHOMA CITY, OK: The Agency for Toxic Substance and Disease Registry found the average birth weight in the Kimsey neighborhood near Tinker Air Force Base to be about two ounces lower than in other Oklahoma City neighborhoods. It attributed the low birth weights to Kimsey residents' greater exposure to chemicals released from the base.

MEMPHIS, TN: The Pentagon's Defense Distribution Depot began operating as a chemical-weapons dump in the heart of Memphis' African-American community in 1942—and didn't warn residents of the danger. The depot contaminated the soil and groundwater. People who live nearby suffer a disproportionate number of miscarriages, birth defects, childhood cancers, and kidney ailments.

SAN ANTONIO, TX: Kelly Air Force Base ranked as the county's fifth-largest air polluter before its 2001 closing. Metals, solvents. and fuel from the base also contaminated the local groundwater. Over 70 former Kelly Air Force Base workers have developed Lou Gehrig's Disease in recent years. The U.S. Agency for Toxic Substance and Disease Registry found elevated levels of cancer, low birth weight, and birth defects in the San Antonio neighborhood closest to the base.

COLONIE, NY: A plant which manufactured 30mm depleted uranium rounds for the U.S. military contaminated a nearby residential community, where the soil was found to contain 500 times more uranium than normal.

CONCORD, MA: Starmet, a company that manufactured depleted uranium ammunition for the U.S. military, contaminated Concord's groundwater and soil with uranium. Local residents have contracted some cancers at rates up to twice those of other Massachusetts residents.

CAPE COD, MA: Toxic pollution from the Massachusetts Military Reservation, former site of Otis Military Base, has contaminated drinking water in the nearby town of Falmouth. Over the years, the military "recycled" old ammunition and hazardous wastes at Otis by openly burning them. It also dumped 6 million gallons of aviation fuel directly on the ground. By 1986, Falmouth's cancer rate was 38% higher than the state average.

ISLA DE VIEQUES, PUERTO RICO: After fifty years of U.S. Navy target practice, Isla de Vieques has more craters per square kilometer than the moon. The Navy's use of bombs, depleted uranium, and Agent Orange on Vieques has produced a cancer rate 26% higher than in the rest of Puerto Rico. Vieques's children also show high levels of mercury and lead. The Navy, which occupies 26,000 of the island's 33,000 acres, has also contaminated the soil, destroyed its coral reefs, and emitted toxic heavy metals into the marine environment.

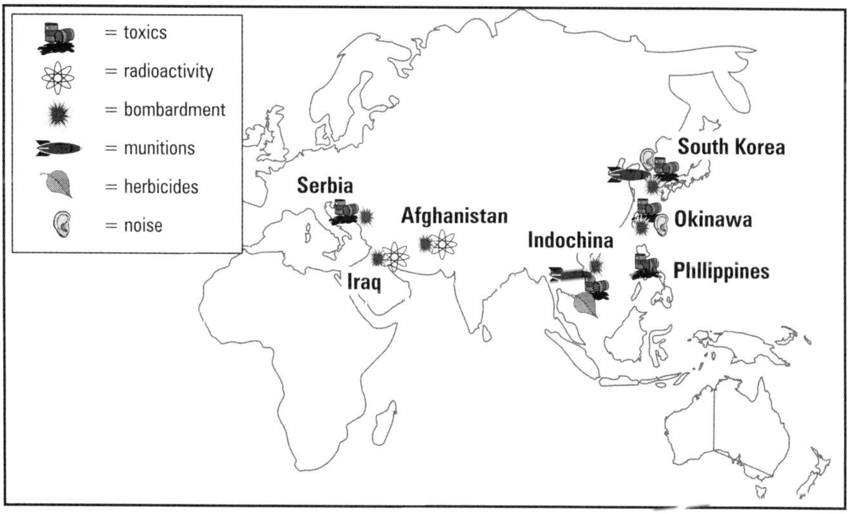

SERBIA: After the U.S. military bombed a petrochemical complex in the suburbs of Belgrade in 1999, the destroyed plastics factory and ammonia production unit released toxins such as chlorine into the air.

IRAQ: U.S. bombing of oil facilities in January 1991 caused spills of 6 to 8 million barrels of crude oil, killing about 30,000 marine birds. For nearly a year afterwards, oil well fires spewed toxic soot. The bombing also poisoned Iraqi water supplies. In addition, according to Iraq's Ministry of Health, depleted uranium from U.S. weapons has contaminated the soil and plants in southern Iraq, causing cancers and deformities associated with uranium exposure.

AFGHANISTAN: Following the Pentagon's 2001-2002 military campaign in Afghanistan, the Uranium Medical Research Center (UMRC) sent two scientific teams to Afghanistan to examine the effects of U.S. bombing on Kabul. Many residents, the UMRC teams found, had symptoms consistent with uranium exposure (joint pains, flu-like illnesses, bleeding mucous membranes, etc.). One fourth of the Kabul newborns examined had health problems consistent with uranium, including lethargy, skin rashes, and enlarged heads.

INDOCHINA: Nearly thirty years after the end of the U.S. war in Southeast Asia, many of the affected ecosystems have still not recovered, according to the Environmental Conference on Cambodia, Laos and Vietnam (Stockholm, 2002). Ten percent of southern Vietnam's forests (including one-third of the coastal mangoes, which play a vital role in the coastal ecosystem and fish habitats) were destroyed by the 72 million liters of herbicide the U.S. military dropped during the Vietnam War era. Arsenic and dioxin in the herbicides are expected to pose a health threat long into the future. Since 1975, 50,000 civilians have been killed by the landmines and other weapons the U.S. military left behind. The U.S.'s vast bombing campaign also left millions of large bomb craters.

SOUTH KOREA: Oil from the Yongsan 8th garrison's base has contaminated the soil and water. Asbestos has been found around the Camp Indian base. In May 1998, a ruptured pipeline at the Mt. Rackun military base polluted a large section of a South Korean forest conservancy area. U.S. military drills and maneuvers have also damaged farmlands and destroyed crops. Oil discharged by the U.S. Army has polluted the Sankogos River, contaminated farmland, and destroyed crops. Off the coast of South Korea, the U.S. military has used small islands as bombing ranges, creating noise pollution for nearby villages. The ammunition left behind has also injured residents.

OKINAWA: U.S. military exercises with live artillery have caused forest fires, soil erosion, and earth tremors—leaving sections of Okinawa barren and shell-ridden. Toxins emitted by the U.S. military have infiltrated Okinawa's land, water and air, and have been linked to low birth weights and elevated rates of leukemia and other cancers. Noise pollution at Kadena Air Base may also be a cause of low birth weights.

PHILIPPINES: The former site of Clark Air Base has contaminated the groundwater. The U.S. military also dumped hazardous waste in a municipal landfill in a residential area of Mabalacat. The power plant at the Subic Bay Naval Base emitted untreated pollutants directly into the air. Toxic waste from the destruction of excess bombs and ammunition were poured into local streams. In addition, most of the sewage generated at the Subic Bay base was discharged each day, untreated, directly into the bay.

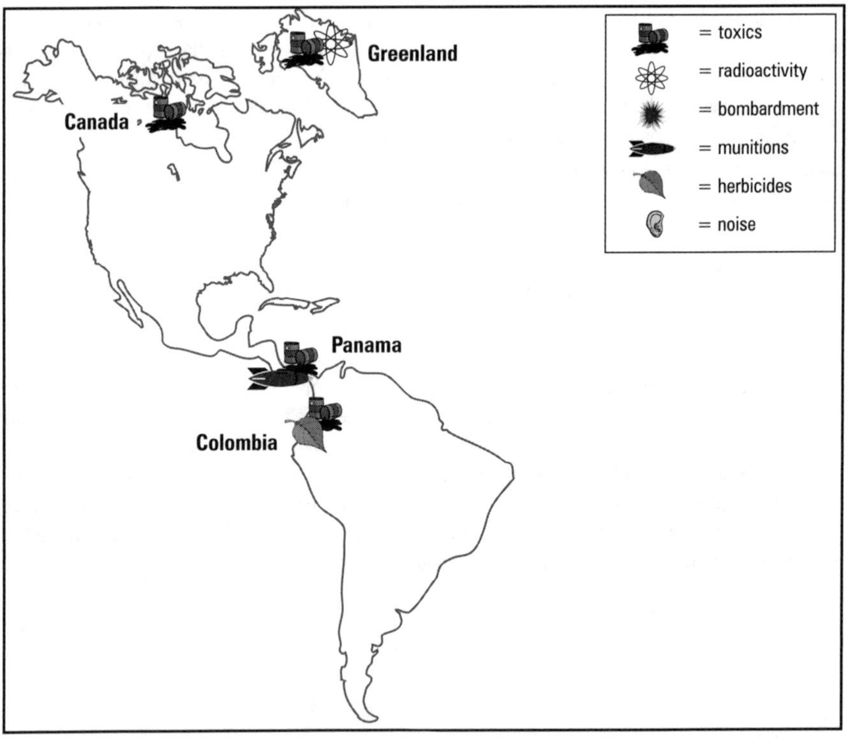

CANADA: The U.S. military built a network of radar sites in Northern Canada between 1953 and 1958. Cancer-causing agents were used in the construction and maintenance of the sites, which are now contaminated.

GREENLAND: In 1968, a B-52 carrying four nuclear bombs crashed near the Pentagon's Thule Air Force base in northern Greenland, causing severe plutonium contamination of the area.

PANAMA: The U.S. military left firing ranges in the Panama Canal Zone littered with thousands of unexploded rounds. A July 1998 Pentagon report found that the U.S. Army Corps of Engineers dumped tons of soil from a project to widen the canal onto 92 acres in Panama's Empire Range, damaging the rainforest ecosystem. A 1997 study for the U.S. Army also discovered the carcinogen TCI in the ground water at Fort Koblhe—at twenty times the level acceptable under U.S. federal law.

COLOMBIA: Large-scale herbicide spraying under the "Plan Colombia"—ostensibly for coca eradication—has caused "serious human health effects; large-scale destruction of food crops; and severe environmental impacts in sensitive tropical ecosystems," according to a 2002 report of the *Aerial Spraying Review*, an environmental publication. There is also evidence that the Pentagon-sponsored fumigation campaign has caused a "loss of agricultural resources, including fish kills and sickness and death of livestock." Border areas of Ecuador have also been contaminated.

IS THE UNITED STATES A POLLUTION HAVEN?

FRANK ACKERMAN

March/April 2003

Free trade, according to its critics, runs the risk of creating pollution havens—countries where lax environmental standards allow dirty industries to expand. Poor countries are the usual suspects; perhaps poverty drives them to desperate strategies, such as specializing in the most polluting industries.

But could the United States be a pollution haven? A look at agriculture under NAFTA, particularly the trade in corn, suggests that at least one polluting industry is thriving in the United States as a result of free trade.

In narrow economic terms, the United States is winning the corn market. U.S. corn exports to Mexico have doubled since 1994, NAFTA's first year, to more than five million tons annually. Cheap U.S. corn is undermining traditional production in Mexico; prices there have dropped 27% in just a few years, and a quarter of the corn consumed in Mexico is now grown in the United States. But in environmental terms, the U.S. victory comes at a great cost.

While the United States may not have more lax environmental standards than Mexico, when it comes to corn U.S. agriculture certainly uses more polluting methods. As it is grown in the United States, corn requires significantly more chemicals per acre than wheat or soybeans, the other two leading field crops. Runoff of excess nitrogen fertilizer causes water pollution, and has created a huge "dead zone" in the Gulf of Mexico around the mouth of the Mississippi River. Intensive application of toxic herbicides and insecticides threatens the health of farm workers, farming communities, and consumers. Genetically modified corn, which now accounts for about one-fifth of U.S. production, poses unknown long-term risks to consumers and to ecosystems.

Growing corn in very dry areas, where irrigation is required, causes more environmental problems. The United States also has a higher percentage of irrigated acreage than Mexico. While the traditional Corn Belt enjoys ample rainfall and does not need irrigation, 15% of U.S. corn acreage—almost all of it in Nebraska, Kansas, the Texas panhandle, and eastern Colorado—is now irrigated. These areas draw water from the Ogallala aquifer, a gigantic underground reservoir, much faster than the aquifer naturally refills. If present rates of overuse continue, the Ogallala, which now contains as much fresh water as Lake Huron, will be drained down to unusable levels within a few decades, causing a crisis for the huge areas of the plains states that depend on it for water supplies. Government subsidies, in years past, helped farmers buy the equipment needed to pump water out of the Ogallala, contributing to the impending crisis.

Moreover, the corn borer, a leading insect pest that likes to eat corn plants, flourishes best in dry climates. Thus the "irrigation states," particularly Texas and Colorado, are the hardest hit by corn borers. Corn growers in dry states have the greatest need for insecticides; they also have the greatest motivation to use genetically modified corn, which is designed to repel corn borers.

Sales to Mexico are particularly important to the United States because many countries are refusing to accept genetically modified corn. Europe no longer imports U.S. corn for this reason, and Japan and several East Asian countries may follow suit. Mexico prohibits growing genetically modified corn, but still allows it to be imported; it is one of the largest remaining markets where U.S. exports are not challenged on this issue.

Despite Mexico's ban, genetically modified corn was recently found growing in a remote rural area in the southern state of Oaxaca. As the ancestral home of corn, Mexico possesses a unique and irreplaceable genetic diversity. Although the extent of the problem is still uncertain, the unplanned and uncontrolled spread of artificially engineered plants from the United States could potentially contaminate Mexico's numerous naturally occurring corn varieties.

An even greater threat is the economic impact of cheap U.S. imports on peasant farmers and rural communities. Traditional farming practices, evolved over thousands of years, use combinations of different natural varieties of corn carefully matched to local conditions. Lose these traditions, and we will lose a living reservoir of biodiversity in the country of origin of one of the world's most important food grains.

The United States has won the North American corn market. But the cost looks increasingly unbearable when viewed through the lens of the U.S. environment, or of Mexico's biodiversity.

GENETIC ENGINEERING AND THE PRIVATIZATION OF SEEDS

ANURADHA MITTAL AND PETER ROSSET

March/April 2001

In 1998, angry farmers burned Monsanto-owned fields in Karnataka, India, starting a nationwide "Cremate Monsanto" campaign. The campaign demanded that biotech corporations like Monsanto, Novartis, and Pioneer leave the country. Farmers particularly targeted Monsanto because its field trials of the "terminator gene"—designed to prevent plants from producing seeds and so to make farmers buy new seed each year—the danger of "genetic pollution" that would sterilize other crops in the area. That year, Indian citizens chose Quit India Day (August 9), the anniversary of Mahatma Gandhi's demand that British colonial rulers leave the country, to launch a "Monsanto Quit India" campaign. Ten thousand citizens from across the country sent the Quit India message to Monsanto's Indian headquarters, accusing the company of colonizing the food system.

In recent years, farmers across the world have echoed the Indian farmers' resistance to the biotech giants. In Brazil, the Landless Workers' Movement (MST) has set out to stop Monsanto soybeans. The MST has vowed to destroy any genetically engineered crops planted in the state of Rio Grande do Sul, where the state government has banned such crops. Meanwhile, last September more than 1,000 local farmers joined a "Long March for Biodiversity" across Thailand. "Rice, corn, and other staple crops, food crops, medicinal plants and all other life forms are significant genetic resources that shape our culture and lifestyle," the farmers declared. "We oppose any plan to transform these into genetically modified organisms."

Industrial Agriculture I: The Green Revolution

For thousands of years, small farmers everywhere have grown food for their local communities—planting diverse crops in healthy soil, recycling organic matter, and following nature's rainfall patterns. Good farming relied upon the farmer's accumulated knowledge of the local environment. Until the 1950s, most Third World agriculture was done this way.

The "Green Revolution" of the 1960s gradually replaced this kind of farming with monocultures (single-crop production) heavily dependent on chemical fertilizers, pesticides, and herbicides. The industrialization of agriculture made Third World countries increase exports to First World markets, in order to earn the foreign exchange they needed to pay for agrochemicals and farm machinery manufactured in the global North. Today, as much as 70% of basic grain production in the global South is the product of industrial farming.

The Green Revolution was an attempt by northern countries to export chemical- and machine-intensive U.S.-style agriculture to the Third World. After the Cuban revolution, northern policymakers worried that rampant hunger created the basis for "communist" revolution. Since the First World had no intention of redistributing the world's wealth, its answer was for First World science to "help" the Third World by giving it the means to produce more food. The Green Revolution was to substitute for the "red."

During the peak Green Revolution years, from 1970 to 1990, world food production per capita rose by 11%. Yet the number of people living in hunger (averaging less than the minimum daily caloric intake) continued to rise. In the Third World—excluding China—the hungry population increased by more than 11%, from 536 to 597 million. While hunger declined somewhat relative to total Third World population, the Green Revolution was certainly not the solution for world hunger that its proponents made it out to be.

Not only did the Green Revolution fail to remedy unequal access to food and food-producing resources, it actually contributed to inequality. The costs of improved seeds and fertilizers hit cash-poor small farmers the hardest. Unable to afford the new technology, many farmers lost their land. Over time, the industrialization of agriculture contributed to the replacement of farms with corporations, farmers with machines, mixed crops with monocultures, and local food security with global commerce.

Industrial Agriculture II: The New Biorevolution

The same companies that promoted chemical-based agriculture are now bringing the world genetically engineered food and agriculture. Some of the leading pesticide companies of yesterday have become what today are euphemistically called "life sciences companies"—Aventis, Novartis, Syngenta, Monsanto, Dupont, and others. Through genetic engineering, these companies are now converting seeds into product-delivery systems. The crops produced by Monsanto's Roundup-Ready brand seeds, for example, tolerate only the company's Roundup brand herbicide.

The "life sciences" companies claim that they can solve the environmental problems of agriculture. For example, they promise to create a world free of pesticides by equipping each crop with its own "insecticidal genes." Many distinguished agriculture scientists, corporate bigwigs, and economists are jumping on the "biotechnology" bandwagon. They argue that, in a world where more than 830 million people go to bed hungry, biotechnology provides the only hope of feeding our burgeoning population, especially in the Third World.

In fact, since genetic engineering is based on the same old principles of industrial agriculture—monoculture, technology, and corporate control—it is likely to exacerbate the problems of ecological and social devastation:

As long as chemical companies dominate the "life sciences" industry, the biotechnology they develop will only reinforce intensive chemical use. Corporations are currently developing plants whose genetic traits can be turned "on" or "off" by applying an external chemical, as well as crops that die if the correct chemical—made by the same company—is not applied.

The biotechnology industry is releasing hundreds of thousands of genetically engineered organisms into the environment every year. These organisms can reproduce, cross-pollinate, mutate, and migrate. Each release of a genetically engineered organism is a round of ecological Russian roulette. Recently, Aventis' genetically engineered StarLink corn, a variety approved by the U.S. Department of Agriculture only for livestock consumption, entered the food supply by mixing in grain elevators and cross-pollination in the field.

With the advent of genetic engineering, corporations are using new "intellectual property" rights to stake far-reaching claims of ownership over a vast array of biological resources. By controlling the ownership of seeds, the corporate giants force farmers to pay yearly for seeds they once saved from each harvest to the next planting. By making seed exchanges between farmers illegal, they also limit farmers' capacity to contribute to agricultural biodiversity.

The False Promise of "Golden Rice"

The biotech industry is taking great pains to advertise the humanitarian applications of genetic engineering. "[M]illions of people—many of them children—have lost their sight to vitamin A deficiency," says the Council for Biotechnology Information, an industry-funded public relations group. "But suppose rice consumers could obtain enough vitamin A and iron simply by eating dietary staples that are locally grown? ... Biotechnology is already producing some of these innovations." More than $10 million was spent over ten years to engineer vitamin A rice—hailed as the "Golden Rice"—at the Institute of Plant Sciences of the Swiss Federal Institute of Technology in Zurich. It will take millions more and another decade of research and development to produce vitamin A rice varieties that can actually be grown in farmers' fields.

In reality, the selling of vitamin A rice as a miracle cure for blindness depends on blindness to lower-cost and safer alternatives. Meat, liver, chicken, eggs, milk, butter, carrots, pumpkins, mangoes, spinach and other leafy green vegetables, and many other foods contain vitamin A. Women farmers in Bengal, an eastern Indian state, plant more than 100 varieties of green leafy vegetables. The promotion of monoculture and rising herbicide use, however, are destroying such sources of vitamin A. For example, bathua, a very popular leafy vegetable in northern India, has been pushed to extinction in areas of intensive herbicide use.

The long-run solutions to vitamin A deficiency—and other nutritional problems—are increased biodiversity in agriculture and increased food security for poor people. In the meantime, there are better, safer, and more economical short-run measures than genetically engineered foods. UNICEF, for example, gives high-dose vitamin A capsules to poor children twice a year. The cost? Just two cents per pill. (You can support the UNICEF Vitamin A project by calling 1-800-FOR-KIDS or visiting <www.unicefusa. org>.)

Intellectual Property Rights and Genetic Engineering

In 1998, Monsanto surprised Saskatchewan farmer Percy Schmeiser by suing him for doing what he has always done and, indeed, what farmers have done for millennia—save seeds for the next planting. Schmeiser is one of hundreds of Canadian and U.S. farmers the company has sued for re-using genetically engineered seeds. Monsanto has patented those seeds, and forbids farmers from saving them.

In recent years, Monsanto has spent over $8.5 billion acquiring seed and biotech companies, and DuPont spent over $9.4 billion to acquire Pioneer Hi-Bred, the world's largest seed company. Seed is the most important link in the food chain. Over 1.4 billion people—primarily poor farmers—depend on farm-saved seed for their livelihoods. While the "gene police" have not yet gone after farmers in the Third World, it is probably only a matter of time.

If corporations like Monsanto have their way, genetic technology—like the so-called "terminator" seeds—will soon render the "gene police" redundant. Far from being designed to increase agricultural production, "terminator" technology is meant to prevent unauthorized production—and increase seed-industry profits. Fortunately, worldwide protests, like the "Monsanto Quit India" campaign, forced the company to put this technology on hold. Unfortunately, Monsanto did not pledge to abandon "terminator" seeds permanently, and other companies continue to develop similar systems.

Future Possible

From the United States to India, small-scale ecological agriculture is proving itself a viable alternative to chemical-intensive and bioengineered agriculture. In the United States, the National Research Council found that "alternative farmers often produce high per acre yields with significant reductions in costs per unit of crop harvested," despite the fact that "many federal policies discourage adoption of alternative practices." The Council concluded that "federal commodity programs must be restructured to help farmers realize the full benefits of the productivity gains possible through alternative practices."

Another study, published in the *American Journal of Alternative Agriculture*, found that ecological farms in India were just as productive and profitable as chemical ones. The author concluded that, if adopted on a national scale, ecological farming would have "no negative impact on food security," and would reduce soil erosion and the depletion of soil fertility while greatly lessening dependence on external inputs.

The country where alternative agriculture has been put to its greatest test, however, is Cuba. Before 1989, Cuba had a model Green Revolution-style agricultural economy (an approach the Soviet Union had promoted as much as the United States). Cuban agriculture featured enormous production units, using vast quantities of imported chemicals and machinery to produce export crops, while the country imported over half its food.

Although the Cuban government's commitment to equity and favorable terms of trade offered by Eastern Europe protected Cubans from undernourishment, the collapse of the East bloc in 1989 exposed the vulnerability of this approach. Cuba plunged into its worst food crisis since the revolution. Consumption of calories and protein dropped by perhaps as much as 30%. Nevertheless, today Cubans are eating almost as well as they did before 1989, with much lower imports of food and agrochemicals. What happened?

Cut off from imports of food and agrochemicals, Cuba turned inward to create a more self-reliant agriculture based on higher crop prices to farmers, smaller production units, urban agriculture, and ecological principles. As a result of the trade embargo, food shortages, and the opening of farmers' markets, farmers began to receive much better prices for their products. Given this incentive to produce, they did so, even without Green Revolution-style inputs. The farmers received a huge boost from the reorientation of government education, research, and assistance toward alternative methods, as well as the rediscovery of traditional farming techniques.

While small farmers and cooperatives increased production, large-scale state farms stagnated. In response, the Cuban government parceled out the state farms to their former employees as smaller-scale production units. Finally, the government mobilized support for a growing urban agriculture movement—small-scale organic farming on vacant lots—which, together with the other changes, transformed Cuban cities and urban diets in just a few years.

Will Biotechnology Feed the World?

The biotech industry pretends concern for hungry people in the Third World, holding up greater food production through genetic engineering as the solution to world hunger. If the Green Revolution has taught us one thing, however, it is that increased food production can—and often does—go hand in hand with more hunger, not less. Hunger in the modern world is not caused by a shortage of food, and cannot be eliminated by producing more. Enough food is already available to provide at least 4.3 pounds of food per person a day worldwide. The root of the hunger problem is not inadequate production but unequal access and distribution. This is why the second Green Revolution promised by the "life sciences" companies is no more likely to end hunger than the first.

The United States is the world's largest producer of surplus food. According to the U.S. Department of Agriculture, however, some 36 million of the country's people (including 14 million children) do not have adequate access to food. That's an increase of six million hungry people since the 1996 welfare reform, with its massive cuts in food stamp programs.

Even the world's "hungry countries" have enough food for all their people right now. In fact, about three quarters of the world's malnourished children live in countries with net food surpluses, much of which are being exported. India, for example, ranks among the top Third World agricultural exporters, and yet more than a third of the world's 830 million hungry people live there. Year after year, Indian governments have managed a sizeable food surplus by depriving the poor of their basic human right to food.

The poorest of the poor in the Third World are landless peasants, many of whom became landless because of policies that favor large, wealthy farmers. The high costs of genetically engineered seeds, "technology-use payments," and other inputs that small farmers will have to use under the new biotech agriculture will tighten the squeeze on already poor farmers, deepening rural poverty. If agriculture can play any role in alleviating hunger, it will only be to the extent that we reverse the existing bias toward wealthier and larger farmers, embrace land reform and sustainable agriculture, reduce inequality, and make small farmers the center of an economically vibrant rural economy.

BETWEEN THE DEVIL AND THE DEEP BLUE SEA

WORKERS IN THE GLOBAL ENVIRONMENT

LAURIE DOUGHERTY

July/August 1999

In 1988, I was recalled to work at General Electric Appliance Park in Louisville, Kentucky, after a four-year layoff. This was not the first long layoff and, as always, getting called back unleashed a complex emotional response. I felt a great rush of relief to be delivered from a series of miserable, low-paying jobs and mounting piles of overdue bills. But I was humiliated that, once again, I hadn't found that perfect job, once again I jumped when GE snapped its fingers.

I was assigned to Building 4, "Refrigeration Components." As jobs went at Appliance Park, this was a good place to work. Building 4 was in the middle of a long and messy restructuring process—moving some work to a nonunion plant and automating production lines while still recovering from a major design screw-up. Workers were transferring to other buildings right and left. As an incentive for workers to stick out the transition, GE raised pay in Building 4. The new systems replaced a lot of people with robots, but it was easier work than the traditional assembly line. And, we got all the overtime we could handle. Despite mixed emotions, I settled in to recover from years of personal fiscal austerity.

But there was a new complication in the emotional mix—environmental disaster on a global scale. Building 4 works on the parts that enable refrigerators to refrigerate, components that circulate the chemicals that withdraw heat from inside the unit and disperse it outside. The refrigerant used at the time was Freon, one of the most prominent chlorofluorocarbons (CFCs)—the class of chemicals responsible for depleting the ozone layer that shields the earth from harmful ultraviolet radiation.

When I went to work in Building 4, the Montreal Protocol on Ozone Depletion was in the final stages of negotiation. No thanks to GE, I was aware of the Montreal Protocol and its implications both for the environment and the appliance industry. From the company I saw only brief mention in the building newsletter of the "challenges" of meeting conflicting government regulations to reduce energy usage and end CFC use. (Substitutes for Freon under consideration were, according to the industry, less efficient and would need more electricity to work effectively.) Later, in an interview with the plant-wide newspaper, a GE executive claimed he had sleepless nights over ozone depletion.

The company was not so passive in its outward stance. The appliance industry lobbied fiercely against the Montreal Protocol. GE's internal indifference and external opposition to the resolution of a major environmental crisis was typical for a company that tops the list of Superfund sites. Ozone depletion was a nonissue among plant workers. Among the workforce, jobs were the only concern. Appliance Park has lost thousands of jobs since I first worked there in 1974 and continues to do so. Building 4 itself has been half empty since GE moved compressor production to a nonunion plant in 1984. I cannot recall any comments from the union about ozone depletion. Once the agreement was passed and the Clean Air Act amendments of 1990 scheduled the phase out of CFCs, GE redesigned its evaporators to comply with new requirements. The company played on the workers' anxiety for all it was worth. Management put the cost of getting evaporators from another source on the table and demanded that the union meet or beat that price in order to keep evaporator production at Appliance Park.

The union won that round, but now, 10 years later, all refrigerator production at Appliance Park is at risk. New energy requirements will become effective in the next few years and GE will have to redesign and retool for a more energy-efficient refrigerator. The union proposed a plan that would cut $30 million from production costs. They are still waiting for a response from the company.

After my experience at Appliance Park (I got laid off in 1991 and never returned), I was not surprised when Pacific Northwest loggers fought against measures to protect old-growth forests or when the AFL-CIO opposed the Kyoto Treaty on global warming. These positions are disappointing, but the issue of jobs versus the environment is not simple to sort out. Recent studies indicate small net job gains from environmental regulation and regulations can open opportunities for jobs in new, environmentally friendly industries. For workers, however, the critical question is not what is the net economic effect of "regulation," but rather, what will happen to my job? This question speaks to a profound anxiety about the loss of livelihood and loss of control—an anxiety that is well grounded in the realities of today's global economy.

The dangers of corporate environmental recklessness are also grounded in reality. More and more labor groups recognize this reality and are attempting to define an agenda that both protects the environment and ensures that workers do not pay a disproportionate part of the costs of transition to an environmentally sound economy. The Work and Environment Initiative (WEI) at Cornell University investigated union efforts on environmental issues. Their report, "Labor and Climate Change and the Environment," published shortly before the December 1997 Kyoto conference on climate change, found that while the labor movement is concerned with protecting its members' jobs, many unions are also deeply concerned about the environment and struggle to reconcile both issues. Workers are, after all, human beings who have to survive on this planet.

Among those most aware of environmental issues are unions involved in environmentally "dirty" industries such as the United Auto Workers. In a particularly forward-thinking resolution, adopted in 1991, the United Steelworkers of America (USWA) called the destruction of the environment potentially the greatest threat to our children and the destruction of the Earth's resource base a serious threat to the economy. Putting this philosophy into practice, in April the Steelworkers filed suit against the California Department of Forestry and Fire Protection challenging the sustained yield plan of the Headwaters Forest agreement with Pacific Lumber. In the press release, USWA spokesperson Jon Youngdahl stated that the plan "authorizes unsustainably high harvests of old growth timber and fails to consider the long-range economic impacts of these unsustainably high harvests."

According to Youngdahl, steelworkers began reaching out to environmentalists in Humboldt County, California, when they realized that the same corporation (Maxxam Corporation) owned both Pacific Lumber and Kaiser Aluminum. Steelworkers have been engaged in a protracted struggle against Kaiser, while environmentalists have long challenged Pacific Lumber's destructive forestry practices. Youngdahl also pointed out that, while the desire to build mutual support against a common enemy forged the initial connection between USWA members and environmentalists, the Headwaters lawsuit goes beyond specific labor disputes to put into action the Steelworkers' long term commitment to sustainability.

Testifying before a hearing on the Sustained Yield Plan, steelworker Don Kegley of Local 338 in Spokane, Washington made a link between the deterioration of Kaiser's record of environmental responsibility since it became part of Maxxam and the danger that another Maxxam company would squander the resources of the Headwaters Forest. Kegley also articulated the link between preserving forest resources for the long term and preserving jobs: "Without the forest, our culture will crumble and worse, our planet will die. And there are no jobs on a dead planet." In May, the USWA and environmental allies took their fight to the Maxxam board meeting.

The Oil, Chemical and Atomic Workers (OCAW), now merged into the Paperworkers, Allied Industrial, Chemical and Energy Workers Union (PACE), has been one of the most environmentally active unions. OCAW was the union involved in the Karen Silkwood case (made famous in the movie *Silkwood*), and has long fought for health and safety on the job. Because they deal with dangerous and environmentally hazardous substances in their workplaces, this union's leaders and members have a heightened consciousness of the ecological impact of their jobs. They have also suffered heavily from deindustrialization in the last few decades and are well aware that workers often bear the brunt of change. Several years ago OCAW proposed a Superfund for workers that would be used to ease workers' transition to more environmentally friendly industries. The Superfund idea has evolved into a campaign for a "Just Transition," and under that banner has begun to reverberate throughout the labor and environmental movements.

Les Leopold of the Labor Institute in New York City, a consultant to OCAW—and now PACE—on environmental issues and himself a PACE member, views "Just Transitions" as a far-reaching program along the lines of the G.I. Bill following World War II. To his mind, it can provide a model for managing workplace change resulting from environmental mandates or the next generation of technology. The key is to provide security and options for workers to move to a new stage of life and work. Older workers may choose to retire early and should be able to do so without loss of income. Other workers may accept subsidized pay to move to lower paying jobs. Still others will return to school to gain up-to-date skills and embark on new careers.

The concept of a "Just Transition" is not confined to the workplace—it embraces communities which suffer both from environmental hazards and economic loss when plants close. One of PACE's most promising programs, from Leopold's point of view, is building connections between the union and environmental justice movement. Minority communities are particularly harmed by being close to polluting factories yet are generally denied the benefits of the high-wage jobs in these industries. PACE is bringing its members together with representatives of the Ponco tribe in Oklahoma, neighbors of oil refineries in southern California, and residents of other endangered communities to develop appreciation of each other's fears and frustrations.

The recent merger that formed PACE is a pivotal event, and is being closely watched by those who care about the emerging Blue Collar-Green Alliance. The merger directly confronts the Paperworkers'—which are traditionally defensive about environmental protection—with the proactive, "do the right thing," stance of OCAW. According the Leopold and also PACE Communication Director, Lynn Baker, the merged union will continue the "Just Transition" programs initiated by OCAW.

The AFL-CIO itself has taken up the struggle for a "Just Transition" and is actively seeking relationships with environmentalists. Soon after taking office, AFL-CIO President John Sweeney appointed Jane Perkins as Environmental Liaison. Perkins has one foot in both labor and environmental worlds. She has been an officer in Service Employees International Union (SEIU) locals, an activist around the Three Mile Island nuclear power plant disaster, and was executive director of the environmental organization Friends of the Earth.

Climate Change now tops Perkins' agenda. The United Mine Workers (UMW), a stronghold of the new AFL-CIO leadership, put climate change on the AFL-CIO's table with resolutions, statements and rallies protesting the Kyoto agreement. UMW members feel especially threatened by initiatives to reduce coal in power generation. Rather than lock horns with environmentalists over specifics of the Kyoto agreement,

Perkins set out to find topics both labor and green groups could discuss productively. Three topics emerged: exploring green technologies on a sector by sector basis; "Just Transitions"; and developing countries. In April of this year, at a two day meeting at the AFL-CIO conference center, Carl Pope, head of the Sierra Club, and Bob Wages, now a PACE official who was a long-time proponent within OCAW of environmental initiatives, were chosen to take the lead in developing a joint strategy on climate change.

The AFL-CIO fears, not without reason, that less stringent caps on carbon emissions in developing countries (at least until the next round of talks), will give them cheaper production costs and, therefore, an advantage in global markets. Although many corporations indeed shift production to low-wage countries in search of lower costs, Ed Cohen-Rosenthal of Cornell's WEI believes that energy costs in the United States will remain comparatively low even when complying with Kyoto requirements.

Developing countries have legitimate grievances with the developed countries which emit the overwhelming majority of greenhouse gases. The standard of living in wealthy countries reflects generations of industrialization, relatively free of environmental restrictions. In the report issued by WEI, Boyd Young of the (then) United Paperworkers International Union argues that it is wrong to regulate only one part of the world. He notes that applying climate change controls to developing countries will provide incentives for them to develop clean energy technologies and reduce the need to retool at a later date. However, the same report summarizes findings of the European Union (EU) Environmental Council which point out that the costs of implementing clean technology are prohibitive for developing countries. The EU Council calls for the developed world to conduct the necessary research and development and to fund vehicles for financing technology transfer to poorer countries. The AFL-CIO's Perkins hopes to involve labor and environmental activists from many countries in putting together a strategy for reducing carbon emissions while protecting workers at the same time.

The International Confederation of Free Trade Unions (ICFTU) and the Trade Union Advisory Committee to the OECD (TUAC) issued a joint statement to the November 1998 Buenos Aires conference on climate change. The ICFTU and TUAC are sympathetic to the dilemmas faced by both developed and developing country workers. Their statement calls for immediate participation on the part of developing countries in reducing carbon emissions, but also states that: "Industrial countries should provide substantial financial and technical assistance as a means of enabling developing countries to adopt binding targets within the context of differentiated goals and long-term implementation strategy." The ICFTU and TUAC claim that the failure to confront employment issues is a major weakness of the Kyoto climate change treaty. But dislocation of workers in energy-intensive sectors of the industrialized world is not the only problem they cite. Workers will also suffer from the failure to check global warming since 70% of the world's population lives and works within 60 kilometers of seacoasts. With global warming on the rise, and ocean levels with it, the potential exists for 60 million environmental refuges by 2030.

Labor organizations point out that workers' knowledge can help create environmental solutions; they know production technology and are in a good position to suggest changes that reduce energy waste and introduce cleaner production options. Many unions, particularly in Europe where there is a tradition of worker participation in decisions affecting workplace conditions, have conducted eco-audits. In these programs, workers evaluate the environmental impact of the materials and techniques they use and recommend ways to reduce waste and institute cleaner processes. The Swedish Confederation of Professional Employees developed a program called The Way to 6E— A Practical Model for Sustainable Workplaces, a blueprint for involving all workers in developing workplace improvements in ergonomics, economy, ecology, emissions, efficiency, and energy.

WEI research confirms the value of workers participation in workplace decisions. In a recent study of toxics, they found that businesses with employee participation programs release fewer toxic substances into the environment than businesses without such programs.

Other programs try to involve communities to reduce pollution that harms both workers and neighborhood residents near industrial sites. The Silicon Valley Toxics Coalition, based in the high tech industry's stronghold, has been a major force in focusing public attention on environmentally unsound practices of the electronics industry.

A recent story in *Sierra*, the 500,000 circulation magazine of the Sierra Club, described the emerging connections between labor and environmentalists as the "coalition that gives corporate polluters fits." The article points out that OCAW, a strong advocate of environmental safety on and off the job, always connected threats to the environment and to workers to the same culprit: corporations. Its "Just Transitions" project is exactly the kind of program that can cut the Gordian knot entangling the issues of jobs and the environment. It demands that the economic burdens of greening industry be shared fairly among all economic actors and has the potential to build a powerful new Blue-Green Alliance to fight for the agenda.

Resources: David Moberg, "Brothers and Sisters—Greens and Labor: It's a Coalition That Gives Polluters Fits," *Sierra* (Jan./Feb., 1999); International Confederation of Trade Unions, various documents at www.icftu.org; Labor Institute, 853 Broadway, NY, NY 10003; Good Neighbors Project, PO Box 79225, Waverly, MA 02179 <www.enviroweb.org/gnp>; Silicon Valley Toxics Coalition, 760 N. First Street, San Jose, CA 95112 <www.svtc.org>.

CHAPTER 3

THE POLITICS AND ECONOMICS OF GLOBAL WARMING

CAR TROUBLE

THE AUTOMOBILE AS AN ENVIRONMENTAL AND HEALTH DISASTER

ALEJANDRO REUSS

March/April 2003

(Scene: Los Angeles, the 1940s)

Eddie Valiant: A freeway? What the hell's a freeway?

Judge Doom: Eight lanes of shimmering cement running from here to Pasadena. Smooth, straight, fast. Traffic jams will be a thing of the past.... I see a place where people get off and on the freeway. On and off. Off and on. All day, all night. Soon where Toontown once stood will be a string of gas stations. Inexpensive motels. Restaurants that serve rapidly prepared food. Tire salons. Automobile dealerships. And wonderful, wonderful billboards reaching as far as the eye can see.... My god, It'll be beautiful.

Eddie Valiant: Come on. Nobody's gonna drive this lousy freeway when they can take the Red Car [trolley] for a nickel.

Judge Doom: Oh, they'll drive. They'll have to. You see, I bought the Red Car so I could dismantle it.

—*Who Framed Roger Rabbit?* (1988)

At the end of *Roger Rabbit*, a speeding train saves the day, destroying the solvent-spraying juggernaut that is set to level the fictitious Toontown for the freeway. In other words, the movie is a fairy tale about how the modern American city *did* not come into existence. In reality, Los Angeles came to represent the awful extreme of the U.S. car culture. Auto companies did buy up the city's Red Car trolley and dismantle it. The landscape became just the cluttered wasteland of highways, fast-food joints, filling stations, and billboards dreamed by the villainous Judge Doom.

The federal government rolled out an asphalt carpet for the automobile: It built the interstate highways that fueled "white flight" to the new suburban sprawl, and carried the new "middle class" on its summer vacations. Soon, freeways criss-crossed American cities, slicing through low-income neighborhoods and consigning commuters to the twice-daily ordeal of gridlock. Roads and highways (along with the military, for which the interstates were originally intended) were politically acceptable objects of public spending even in the postwar United States. And why not? They represented an enormous subsidy to the private industries at the heart of U.S. capitalism—oil, steel, and cars.

The car effectively privatized a wide swath of the public arena. In place of the city square, it created the four-way intersection. Instead of walking or riding a trolley, the motorists sealed themselves inside their individual steel cocoons. Cars offered convenience—for grocery shopping, trips to the mall, chauffeuring the kids to school and practice, etc.—to those who got them. Their real triumph, however, was to manufacture inconvenience for those who didn't. People who could not afford cars had such unenviable choices as navigating the brave new world of speeding traffic on foot or waiting for the bus. A genuine political commitment to public transportation might have lessened the class and race divide. Most public transportation funding, however, has gone to road and highway construction geared to the motorist, and much of what remains for mass transit has been devoted to commuter trains serving the suburban middle class. Low-income city residents have largely been abandoned to an infrequent and polluting diesel bus.

As it turned out, life inside the car was not all it was cracked up to be either—especially when traffic on the freeway slowed to a crawl. In gridlock, you can practically see the steam coming out of drivers' ears. As odious as much of the time spent in cars might be, however, Americans have learned, or been convinced, to "love the car." It has become a fetish object—a symbol of freedom and individualism, power and sex appeal. The commercials always seem to show a carefree motorist speeding through the countryside or climbing a secluded mountain to gaze on the landscape below. Fortunately, not too many SUV owners actually spend their time tearing up the wilderness. Unfortunately, they spend much of it spewing exhaust into the city air.

The SUV certainly ranks among the more absurd expressions of American overconsumption (General Motors' Yukon XL Denali, to cite an extreme example, is over 18 feet long and weighs about three tons). But it is too easy to condemn this overgrown behemoth and then hop self-satisfied back into a midsize sedan. Most of what is wrong with the SUV—the resources it swallows, the dangers it poses, and the blight it creates—is wrong with the automobile system as a whole. Automobiles pollute the oceans and the air, overheat cities and the earth, devour land and time, produce waste and noise, and cause injury and illness.

Here, in more detail, is an indictment of the car as an environmental and public-health menace:

The Bill of Particulars

Oil Pollution

Transportation accounts for over two-thirds of U.S. oil consumption, according to the Department of Energy. The problem of oil pollution, therefore, lands squarely at the doorstep of a transportation system based on internal combustion. Oil tanker spills are the most visible scourge of the world's oceans. According to the National Research Council study Oil in the Sea, tankers spew 400 million tons of oil into the world's oceans each year. Technologies to prevent or contain oil spills, however, cannot solve the problem of marine oil pollution, since the main cause is not spills, but the consumption of oil. Urban consumption, including runoff from roads and used motor oil just poured down the drain, accounts for more than half of the ocean pollution, over one billion tons of oil annually. That does not count, of course, oil that does not make it to the seas, that stains roadways, contaminates the land, or spoils fresh water supplies.

Air Pollution

Automotive emissions are a major source of ozone and carbon monoxide pollution. "[I]n numerous cities across the country," according to the Environmental Protection Agency (EPA), "the personal automobile is the single greatest polluter." Ozone, a major component of urban smog, is formed by unburned fuel reacting with other compounds in the atmosphere. It causes irritation of the eyes and lungs, aggravates respiratory problems, and can damage lung tissue. Researchers at the Centers for Disease Control in Atlanta took advantage of temporary traffic reduction during the 1996 Olympic Games to observe the effects of automotive emissions on asthma attacks. Their study, published in the Journal of the American Medical Association, showed a 28% reduction of peak ozone levels and an 11-44% drop in the number of children requiring acute asthma care (depending on the sample). Carbon monoxide, formed by incomplete burning of fuel, impairs the oxygen-carrying ability of the blood. According to the EPA, "In urban areas, the motor vehicle contribution to carbon monoxide pollution can exceed 90 percent." A 2002 study published in the journal Circulation showed a link between automotive exhaust and heart attacks, and Harvard Medical School researchers called exhaust an "insidious contributor to heart disease."

Climate Change

Automotive exhaust also contains carbon dioxide, a "greenhouse gas" and the principal culprit in climate change (or "global warming"). It is produced, in the words of the EPA, by the "perfect combustion" of hydrocarbons. Internal combustion engines generate this greenhouse gas no matter how efficient or well-tuned they may be. In the United States, the country with the world's highest per capita carbon dioxide emissions, transportation accounts for over 30% of total emissions, according to a 1998 report of the United Nations Framework Convention on Climate Change. More than half that amount, reports the EPA, is due to personal transportation. As average fuel efficiency gets worse (it declined by nearly 7% between 1987 and 1997) and U.S. motorists rack up more vehicle miles (they increased by a third over the same period), the automobile contributes more and more to global warming.

Heat Islands

The temperature in a major city on a summer day can be as much as 8°F higher than that of surrounding rural areas, according to the Berkeley National Laboratory's Heat Island Group. The automobile contributes to "heat islands" mainly through increased demand for roads and parking. The asphalt and concrete used for these surfaces are among the most heat-absorbent materials in the urban environment. Paving also contributes to the loss of trees, which provide shade and dissipate heat. In the 1930s, when orchards dotted Los Angeles, summer temperatures peaked at 97°F, according to the Heat Island Group. Since then L.A. has become one of the country's worst heat islands, with summer temperatures reaching over 105°F. This does not just make the city less pleasant in the summertime. Heat islands cause increased energy use for cooling and increased ozone formation. Researchers estimate a 2% increase in Los Angeles's total power use and a 3% increase in smog for every 1°F increase in the city's daily high temperature.

Land Use

Cars occupy a huge amount of space. Paved roads occupy over 13,000 square miles of land area across the United States—nearly 750 square meters per U.S. motor vehicle—and parking occupies another 3,000 square miles, according to a report by Todd Litman of the Victoria Transport Policy Institute. In urban areas, roads and parking take up 20-30% of the total surface area; in commercial districts, 50-60%. When moving, vehicles require a "buffer zone" that varies with size and speed. Litman calculates, for example, that a pedestrian walking at 3 miles per hour (m.p.h.) requires 20 square feet of space. A cyclist riding at 10 m.p.h. needs 50 square feet. At full occupancy, a bus traveling at 30 m.p.h. requires 75 square feet per passenger. Meanwhile, a car traveling at 30 m.p.h. demands 1,500 square feet. In short, much of the road space is not required by on-road transportation as such, but by the private car. The same goes for parking space. A parked car requires twenty times the space as a parked bicycle, and eighty times the space as a person.

Materials

In the words of the EPA, "Vehicles require a lot of energy and materials to make, consume a lot of energy when used, and present unique waste disposal challenges at end-of-life." The auto industry uses nearly two thirds of the rubber, over one third of the iron, and over one fourth of the aluminum produced in the United States. Over ten million cars, moreover, are junked in the United States each year. About three fourths of the average car's weight—including the vast majority of the steel—is recycled. The rest crowds garbage dumps and contributes to toxic pollution. About 270 million tires (about 3.4 million tons) are scrapped in the United States annually. While nearly half are burned for energy, about 500 million tires now swell U.S. junk piles, where they "act as breeding grounds for rats and mosquitoes," according to the EPA, and periodically erupt into toxic tire fires. The U.S. cars scrapped each year also contain upwards of 8 tons of mercury. Meanwhile, polyvinyl chloride from scrap cars produces dioxins and other toxic pollutants. The study End-of-Life Vehicles: A Threat to the Environment concludes that the cars scrapped in Europe each year (75-85% as many as in the United States) produce 2 million tons of hazardous waste, about one tenth of the EU's total hazardous waste production.

Time

Car travel swallows more and more time as commutes grow longer and congestion more severe. The 2002 Urban Mobility Report from the Texas Transportation Institute calculated, on the basis of data from 75 U.S. cities, that the average motorist wasted 62 hours per year sitting in rush-hour traffic. (That's just the difference between rush-hour travel time and the normal time required to make the same trip.) In Los Angeles, the figure reached 136 hours. All told, over one third of the average rush-hour trip in the very large cities surveyed was wasted on traffic congestion. How is that an environmental or health issue? According to report Transport, Environment, and Health, issued by the World Health Organization (WHO) Regional Office for Europe, studies have connected traffic congestion with increased stress and blood pressure, as well as "aggressive behavior and increased likelihood of involvement in a crash."

Activity

Lack of exercise contributes to coronary heart disease, hypertension, some cancers, osteoporosis, poor coordination and stamina, and low self-esteem. The WHO Regional Office for Europe argues that "walking and cycling as part of daily activities should become a major pillar" of public-health strategy, and that daily travel offers the most promise to "integrate physical activities into daily schedules." Car dependence, instead, extends the sedentary lifestyle even to mobility. Half of all car trips in Europe, according to the WHO Regional Office, are under 5 km, distances most people can cover by bicycle in less than 20 minutes and on foot in well under one hour. High levels of automotive traffic, moreover, may deter people from walking or cycling—due to the unpleasantness of auto exhaust, the fear of crossing fast-moving traffic, or the dangers of riding a bicycle surrounded by cars. Some people may substitute car trips, but those without access to cars (especially children and elderly people) may simply venture outside less frequently, contributing to social isolation (another health risk factor).

Noise

Noise pollution is no mere nuisance. Researchers are beginning to document the damage that noise, even at relatively low levels, can do to human health. A 2001 study by Gary Evans of Cornell University, for example, has shown that children chronically exposed to low-level traffic noise suffer elevated blood pressure, increased changes in heart rate when stressed, and higher overall levels of stress-related hormones. In a separate study, on children exposed to low-level noise from aircraft flight patterns, Evans also documented negative effects of noise pollution on children's attention spans and learning abilities.

Collisions

Finally, the car crash ranks among the leading causes of death and injury in the United States. The statistics for 2001, compiled by the National Highway Traffic Safety Administration, were typical: over 42,000 people killed, over 360,000 people suffering incapacitating injuries, and over 3 million people injured overall. Over the last 25 years, the number of people killed per vehicle mile has declined by over 50%—undoubtedly thanks to such factors as increased availability and use of safety belts and airbags, improved vehicle design, and improved trauma care. The absolute number of deaths, however, has decreased by less than 20% (using the benchmark of 51,000 in 1980), as total vehicle miles traveled have more than doubled. Overall, the U.S. death toll from car crashes over the last quarter century is over one million people. During just the last decade, the total number of people injured in U.S. car crashes has topped 32 million.

The Path of Redemption

The environmental and public-health problems associated with the automobile have often inspired well-meaning exhortations to car-pool, drive less, or drive smaller cars, as well as dreams of "cars of the future" requiring less material or burning cleaner fuels. On the whole, however, the problems are neither individual nor technological—but social. So no individual nor technological solution will do. A comprehensive solution requires turning the "machine space" built for and dominated by the car back into human space: In the place of sprawl, compact development with work, school, stores, and recreation nearby and reachable without a car. In the place of the private car, reliable, clean, and accessible public transportation (along with small, efficient, non-polluting vehicles for those who need them). In the place of internal combustion, the cyclist and the pedestrian—no longer marginalized and endangered, but respected as integral parts of a new, sustainable transportation system.

Cuba and China are the world's leading countries in bicycle use. Even in the rich capitalist counties, however, there are islands of sanity where public and human-powered transportation exist at least on a par with the automobile. Groningen, the Netherlands' sixth-largest city, suggests the possibilities: low speed limits reduce the dangers of urban traffic to cyclists and pedestrians; cars are not permitted on some streets, while bicycles can travel on any public way (including bike only lanes and paths); parking for cars is restricted to garages, while secure bicycle parking facilities are plentiful (especially near train stations); cars are excluded from all squares in the city center, while careful city planning ensures that places of work and commerce are accessible to public transportation, cyclists, and pedestrians. As a result, Groningen residents now make nearly half of all in-city trips by bicycle; less than one third by car. The Dutch city of Delft, and the German cities of Freiburg and Muenster, are similar harbingers of a possible sustainable future.

The sustainable-transportation movement has shown encouraging worldwide growth in recent years. Transportation activists in the United Kingdom have carried out direct-action "street takings," closing off roads and highways and prompting spontaneous street fairs, to show what a car free future might look like. The "Critical Mass" movement, starting in San Francisco in 1992 but quickly spreading to other cities, has brought together cyclists for rolling protest "marches" against auto hegemony. Activists have promoted worldwide car-free days, in which residents of hundreds of cities have participated. Bogotá, Colombia, a city of 7 million, held its first annual car-free day in 2000, complete with fines for any motorists caught within the city limits. Its popularity among city residents has bolstered long-term plans to exclude cars from the city, on a permanent basis, during peak morning and afternoon travel hours. In 2002, Seattle became the first U.S. city to officially host a car-free day.

With greater struggle, a more thorough-going transportation reform might be possible even within the confines of capitalism. This would require, however, a colossal economic shift—away the production of private automobiles, gasoline, and roads, and toward the reconstruction of public transportation and public space in general. It's highly unlikely, considering the ruin of former auto production centers like Detroit and Flint, that the "free market" could manage such a shift without imposing a wrenching dislocation on individuals and communities dependent on auto production. Moreover, it's virtually unimaginable, considering the trends toward privatization and commodification rampant in contemporary capitalism, that it would carry out such a transformation spontaneously.

GLOBAL WARMING

HOW BIG BUSINESS CONTROLS THE DEBATE IN THE U.S.— NOT TO WORRY, SAY U.S. LOBBYISTS

DAVID LEVY

November/December 1997

Delegates from around the world are preparing for December meetings in Kyoto, Japan to finalize an agreement limiting emissions of greenhouse gases. But industry associations representing large producers and users of fossil fuels are gearing up for a massive advertising campaign, intended to convince the public and policy makers that an emissions treaty would be an economic disaster.

Despite an emerging consensus among scientists that higher atmospheric levels of gases such as carbon dioxide are gradually warming the earth's climate, raising sea levels and causing more extreme weather patterns, many businesses seem more concerned with the threat to their bottom lines than with the environment. Yet some other companies believe that they can profit handsomely from controlling emissions.

In July 1996, the United States reversed its long-standing opposition to mandatory international controls on greenhouse gases, but made clear it would only support modest cuts with long time frames. The Clinton administration's statement sought to assure business that any measures would not be "economically disruptive" and would employ "the genius of the private sector" to find "market-based solutions that are flexible and cost-effective."

One of the most powerful lobbies opposing action on global warming is the Global Climate Coalition (GCC), which represents more than 50 companies and trade associations in the oil, coal, utility, chemical, and auto industries. These industries stand to lose out if curbs are placed on fossil fuels, and so the GCC has spent nearly $1 million a year to convince policy makers that proposals to limit CO_2 emissions "are premature and are not justified by the state of scientific knowledge or the economic risks they create."

Political action committees (PACs) sponsored by members of the GCC have contributed millions of dollars to congressional candidates. The GCC has participated in efforts to challenge the scientific predictions of global warming, and has commissioned several reports that emphasize the economic costs of measures to address climate change.

The Global Climate Information Project, whose sponsors include the National Association of Manufacturers, Air Transport Association of America, National Cattlemen's Beef Association and United Mine Workers of America, says it already has spent $3 million on a campaign against the treaty, and its spending could exceed $13 million over the next few months. The Project warns of a "50-cent-per-gallon gasoline tax and higher prices for everything from heat to food to clothing."

Nearly 2,000 respected scientists from around the world concluded in a 1996 report commissioned by the United Nations that human activity was contributing to global warming. But the GCC and the Climate Council, another association representing oil and coal interests, claim that Drs. Benjamin Santer and Tom Wigley, the two lead authors, deleted passages that dissented or expressed uncertainty. While these efforts to discredit the science of climate change have fallen flat in the international negotiations, they have had a powerful impact in the United States. In a series of congressional hearings in 1995 and 1996, the testimony of a few "climate skeptics," several of whom receive funding from industry, created the impression of considerable scientific uncertainty.

After one of the hearings, Dana Rohrabacher from California, chair of the House Science Subcommittee on Energy and Environment, derided climate change research as "liberal claptrap," and was instrumental in cutting funding for further research. Western Fuels, an association of U.S. utilities, has even claimed that climate change is good for the environment because "CO_2 fertilization of the atmosphere helps produce more food for people and wildlife." This association spent about $250,000 to produce a video in 1991 called "The Greening of Planet Earth," which was apparently influential in the Bush administration.

The Clinton administration's recent announcement that it would support mandatory emissions limits generated an outburst of indignation from the Global Climate Coalition. But the new U.S. policy reflects emerging common ground in business sectors that are less directly tied to fossil fuels. Indeed, many companies could benefit from the development of new low-emission technologies and products.

One industry association that has been lobbying for an international treaty is the Business Council for Sustainable Energy, which represents companies in natural gas (a relatively low carbon fuel), energy efficiency, and renewable energy. This association has been pushing for the federal government to provide subsidies for low-carbon alternatives and to encourage export markets for new technologies and products in developing countries. Compared to the GCC, however, the BCSE comprises relatively small companies in fragmented industries, so its political leverage is limited.

Perhaps more instrumental in turning around the U.S. position has been the work of the International Climate Change Partnership (ICCP), a large industry association representing a broad range of manufacturing interests. Some of these companies have divisions that manufacture insulation and efficiency equipment and could benefit from curbs on fossil fuels, while others are still concerned about the impact of higher energy costs. General Electric's gas turbine business could benefit from a switch away from coal, but its appliance and aircraft divisions could be hurt by emissions controls. AT&T is promoting telecommuting as an approach to reducing emissions from transportation. The energy company Enron has substantial interests in gas power generation and has recently invested in a joint venture with Amoco to produce photovoltaic panels.

The ICCP has tried to position itself as the "responsible middle ground" in the negotiations. It has tentatively accepted the need for some control measures, but wants to make sure that key businesses are part of designing any treaty, in order to give them the opportunity to develop and market appropriate new products and processes.

The United States is not the only country where business interests speak louder than environmental concerns. Members of OPEC, led by Saudi Arabia and Kuwait, have (not surprisingly) been among the most vociferous opponents of any restrictions. Much of the developing world, which already accounts for an estimated 45% of total greenhouse gas emissions, has been firmly opposed to any agreement. They believe that the rich countries are primarily responsible for existing carbon dioxide levels, and that cheap energy is needed to fuel growth. China, with one-third of the world's proven reserves of coal, relies on coal for around 80% of its energy needs and plans to expand its coal production fivefold by 2020. Brazil, Indonesia, and Malaysia, home to much of the world's tropical rain forest, have expressed concern that a treaty might limit their ability to log and export timber, or to clear land for agricultural use.

In Europe, France has been relatively supportive of emission controls because it already obtains more than 60% of its electricity from nuclear plants, and hopes that controls on fossil fuels might spur exports of its nuclear technology. Germany, the strongest European advocate of strict controls, has been rapidly reducing its dependence on coal due to concerns about acid rain and the cost of coal subsidies, which exceeded $4 billion a year in the 1980s. Germany has been able to reduce emissions by closing inefficient plants in the former East Germany, and possesses a relatively strong renewable energy sector. The United Kingdom followed the U.S. position against controls until the early 1990s. But then-Prime Minister Margaret Thatcher, not generally known for her dedication to the environmental cause, used the climate change issue to justify the wholesale closing of coal pits. In the process she undermined the National Union of Miners, one of the last bastions of radical unionism in the country.

As Kyoto nears, the international community is looking to the United States, the world's largest emitter of greenhouse gases, for leadership. Environmental groups are also gearing up for a fight. The U.S.-based group Ozone Action has been publicizing the corporate links of the "climate skeptics" and a coalition of environmental groups is planning its own advertising campaign with the theme "This weather report is brought to you by a major corporation." Bill Clinton, meanwhile, has refused to commit to any specific reduction goals, and appears reluctant to move without the assent of two key industries, oil and automobiles. That's industrial democracy at work.

Resources: *The Heat Is On*, Ross Gelbspan, 1997; "Business and International Environmental Treaties," David L. Levy, *California Management Review* 39:3 (Spring 1997).

BUSINESS AND CLIMATE CHANGE

PRIVATIZING ENVIRONMENTAL REGULATION?

DAVID L. LEVY

January/February 2001

Human-caused emissions of greenhouse gases have "contributed substantially to the observed warming over the past 50 years" and, if left unchecked, could cause the earth's average surface temperature to rise between 2.7 and 11 degrees Fahrenheit. So concluded an October 2000 report of the Intergovernmental Panel on Climate Change (IPCC), the international group of scientists charged with assessing the causes, extent, and impact of climate change. The IPCC's language is much stronger than in its previous report, issued five years ago, and the range of warming is nearly twice the previous estimate. Industries dependent on fossil fuels, however, did not react to the 2000 report with the stonewalling that once typified their public declarations on climate change.

Before the November 1997 Kyoto Protocol, an international agreement which established mandatory limits on the emission of greenhouse gases, large sectors of U.S. industry waged an intense and well-funded campaign against international regulation. Companies organized a strong industry association, the Global Climate Coalition (GCC), challenging the scientific basis for action and highlighting the economic costs of curtailing emissions. In the months leading up to the meeting of more than 150 country delegates in Kyoto, U.S. industry put $13 million into the Global Climate Information Project, a public relations campaign against any international agreement.

Even before Kyoto, however, the first signs of a major shift were visible in Europe. In May 1997, John Browne, the Group Chief Executive of oil giant British Petroleum (BP), declared publicly, "The time to consider the policy dimensions of climate change is not when the link between greenhouse gases and climate change is conclusively proven, but when the possibility cannot be discounted and is taken seriously by the society of which we are part." By 1998, U.S. industry was also showing a change in stance. The GCC was weakened by a series of defections: BP left in late 1997, Shell in April 1998, and Ford in December 1999. In 1998, General Motors (GM) joined an initiative of the World Resources Institute called "Safe Climate, Sound Business," agreeing that precautionary action should be taken on climate change. That same year, 13 companies, including BP, Toyota, Boeing, Lockheed, and Enron, joined the newly formed Pew Center on Global Climate Change. The companies endorsed a series of newspaper advertisements stating that they "accept the views of most scientists that enough is known about the science and environmental impacts of climate change for us to take actions to address its consequences."

Smoke and Mirrors?

Many environmentalists doubt the sincerity of big business's sudden conversion. Given the history of industry hostility to emission controls, changed public statements can easily be dismissed as cynical posturing or "greenwashing." In May 1999, for example, William Clay Ford, Jr., the new chairman of Ford Motor Company, proclaimed that "more and more, the marketplace will demand vehicles that are truly clean." At the same time, Ford continued to produce ever larger trucks and sports utilities vehicles (SUVs), like the 12-mile-per-gallon Expedition, contributing to the continuing decline in U.S. fuel economy. Even Shell and BP, the apostles of the new movement, have not curtailed their oil exploration or refining activities at all. The $100 million a year Shell has pledged to invest in renewables is only about 7% of the company's total annual expenditure on petroleum exploration and production.

Incomplete though the conversion may be, investments of hundreds of millions of dollars cannot be discounted as mere public relations. Since its acquisition of Amoco, BP has become the world's largest producer of solar photovoltaic panels, with plans to reach $1 billion in sales by 2010. Shell has also announced that it will invest $500 million in photovoltaics over five years as part of a new International Renewable Energy Division. In 1998, European automakers (including European subsidiaries of U.S.-based companies) accepted a "voluntary" agreement to reduce carbon emissions by about 25% over the following decade. European car companies have introduced very small, light-weight cars, like Daimler-Chrysler's SMART car, and invested substantial amounts in a range of technologies from diesel to fuel cells. Even the most ardent opponents of mandatory emission controls have begun to invest in low-emission technologies. In December 1997, Ford invested about $400 million in a fuel-cell joint venture with Daimler-Chrysler and the Canadian company Ballard. Texaco was the first major U.S. oil company to break ranks and proclaim the need for precautionary action on climate, and in May 2000 it invested $67 million in Electronic Conversion Devices, a company which develops advanced batteries and solar technology.

This shift suggests something more than mere PR "greenwashing," though less than a conversion to sustainable practice. It is not surprising that large sectors of industry viewed action on climate change as a major stategic threat. Controls on the emission of carbon dioxide, the main greenhouse gas, would raise the price of fuels and hurt the revenues and profits of oil, coal, and car companies, as well as other energy-intensive industries. The companies seem to have concluded, however, that open defiance of the climate-change consensus could jeopardize their long-run interests even more—causing them to lose political legitimacy and therefore the power to shape the eventual regulatory outcome. This change of attitude illustrates the resilience of capitalism and the strategies by which business attempts to sustain hegemony—dominance based on consent, the projection of moral leadership, and an ability to present one's goals as the general interest. In the face of strong challenges from state institutions and civil society, companies are moving away from confrontation, and instead towards a strategy of accommodation, compromise, and cooptation.

Explaining the Turnaround

The change in Europe can be understood mostly as a response to political and social pressures. From a European perspective, the ratification of the Kyoto Protocol and the imposition of mandatory emission controls appear inevitable. European firms were concerned that, if they aggressively opposed emission controls, they might be jeopardizing their privileged access and influence with policymakers. In international negotiations, the European Union has called for bigger emission cuts than the United States, and European politicians were sensitive to charges that they talked tough but lacked the will to act. Therefore, they looked to industry for substantial, early emission reductions. The auto industry was already on the defensive for environmental reasons, even facing a total ban on cars in some cities. This complex of factors resulted in the European car industry's agreement to the "voluntary" emission reductions.

U.S. companies, meanwhile, have experienced growing pressure to respond to their competitors' moves in other countries. In the auto industry, Ford and GM saw Toyota launch the Prius, a hybrid electric-gasoline engine car, in Japan in 1998 and the United States in 2000. Honda leapfrogged Toyota, launching its own hybrid, Insight, in the U.S. market in December 1999. While U.S. companies publicly expressed skepticism about the market potential for small, expensive, fuel-efficient cars, they stepped up their own plans for low-emission technologies. Companies often prefer to make mistakes together rather than risk ceding a major advantage to competitors. After Daimler-Chrysler announced a target date of 2004 for introducing a commercial fuel cell vehicle, Ford, GM, BMW, and Honda followed with similar announcements. Ford's and GM's European subsidiaries had already agreed to substantial emission cuts, so these companies needed to develop the appropriate technologies anyway. When Ford announced in the spring of 2000 that it would improve the fuel economy of its SUVs by 25%, GM quickly followed suit.

Within the GCC, more companies were questioning the value of aggressively denying the climate problem. The public effort to challenge the legitimacy of the IPCC had little impact, and even threatened to backfire on industry. Environmental groups in Europe and the United States seized upon the lobbying and public relations efforts of the fossil fuel industry, issued a number of reports that documented industry support for climate skeptics, and attempted to frame the issue as big business using its money and power to distort the scientific debate. In the run-up to the Kyoto conference in December 1997, the GCC decided to shift strategy. Instead of challenging the science, industry's message shifted to the high cost and limited environmental effectiveness of an agreement that excludes developing countries from emission controls. After Kyoto, companies increasingly worried that they were losing political access. The Pew Center's Eileen Claussen was blunt in stating that "joining Pew gives companies credibility, and credibility means political access and influence."

In the years since Kyoto, companies have begun to reevaluate the threat posed to their economic interests by emission controls. In the oil industry, companies have come to realize that their primary markets for oil and gas will enjoy significant growth for at least 20 years. Rapid growth of car ownership in developing countries and the continued growth of vehicle-miles traveled in industrialized countries will offset the gradual introduction of low-emission car technologies. With global air travel growing at about 5% annually, aviation remains a strong market for the oil industry. Demand for natural gas, a relatively low-carbon fuel, is also booming worldwide, as small, efficient gas turbines replace large coal-fired electric power plants. In the auto industry, companies are realizing that they can stay in the business of making and selling cars, even if the engine undergoes radical change. Change is likely to be slow, in any event, because new technologies are expensive and could require massive investments in alternative fuel infrastructure.

The likelihood of stringent emission controls in the short term has also receded. Parties to the Kyoto Protocol only reached agreement in 1997 by deferring difficult decisions about implementation. It has therefore become easier for companies to win public sympathy and political credibility by expressing support for a weak and ineffective international treaty. As details have emerged, companies have realized that there will be plenty of room for fudging. The United States is planning to comply with its commitments on emissions by buying emissions credits from other countries. Russia and other East European countries, whose economies collapsed along with the Soviet Union, now emit far less carbon dioxide than in the 1990 baseline year, allowing them to sell billions of tons of carbon credits, labeled "hot air" by critics. The United States has resisted European efforts to restrict the percentage of a country's commitments that can be met by emissions trading. It has also pushed for credits rewarding hard-to-measure increases in "carbon uptake" (due to such factors as expanded forest lands).

There is still some danger that the whole process could collapse. It is becoming clear that even the modest emission-reduction targets established in Kyoto are unlikely to be met. The United States agreed to reduce emissions to 7% below 1990 levels by the "budget period" 2008-2012, but by 1999 its emissions were already 13.1% above 1990 levels. Although an agreement was reached in Kyoto, industry efforts have succeeded in blocking its ratification by the U.S. Senate. The Senate is unlikely to ratify the treaty without major revisions, which will be opposed by most other countries. Without the participation of the United States, which accounts for nearly one-quarter of global emissions, the Kyoto Protocol is meaningless. According to one anonymous industry source, the GCC did not collapse; it was more a case of "mission accomplished; now we can avoid the political cost of membership."

The Privatization of International Environmental Governance

Even as some environmentalists have welcomed industry's changed stance on climate change, some observers have expressed concern that increasing industry participation in shaping regulation amounts to the privatization of environmental governance. In fact, industry has been closely involved in international climate policy from the outset. The Business Council for Sustainable Development, a group of industrialists representing 48 of the world's largest multinational corporations, was particularly active at the UN Rio conference in 1992, and helped to ensure that the original Framework Convention on Climate Change contained no binding commitments.

Governments have encouraged industry involvement. In a 1996 speech announcing that the United States would no longer oppose binding international emission controls, U.S. State Department negotiator Tim Wirth proclaimed that "meeting this challenge requires that the genius of the private sector be brought to bear on the challenge of developing the technologies that are necessary to ensure our long term environmental and economic prosperity." The U.S. Environmental Protection Agency and Department of Energy have adopted the same stance. The Climate Wise program, jointly administered by the two agencies, bills itself as "a unique partnership that can help you turn energy efficiency and environmental performance into a corporate asset." At the international level, IPPC head Bob Watson attempted to head off criticism of its 2000 report by recruiting corporate experts as chapter authors and reviewers.

In the absence of an international mechanism to limit emissions, private bodies have been taking the initiative. The World Bank Prototype Carbon Fund (PCF) was established in 2000 as "public-private partnership" between a few national governments, including the Netherlands, Sweden, Japan, and Canada, and 26 companies, including Hydro Quebec, Daimler-Chrysler, Shell-Canada, BP-Amoco, and numerous Japanese firms. The Fund's purpose is to raise $140 million for investments in renewables and efficiency in developing countries, projects that will earn carbon credits for the investing companies. The Environmental Defense Fund (EDF) brought together seven large companies, including Dupont, Alcan, Shell and BP, in the summer of 2000 to form the "Partnership for Climate Action," whose purpose is to enable emission trading among its members.

The Price of Accommodation

Compared to the history of corporate denial and hostility, these moves appear to be constructive and proactive. The cost of this accommodation and compromise with industry, however, is a loss of democratic process and accountability. Dan Becker of the Sierra Club has sharply criticized the EDF's emissions trading initiative, saying it offered only modest reductions in greenhouse gases while undercutting efforts to write strong regulations on emission controls as part of the 1997 Kyoto treaty. Peter Utting, in a UN report called "Business Responsibility for Sustainable Development," concluded that "the most significant concern with some forms of voluntary initiatives and partnerships is that they may serve to weaken key drivers of corporate responsibility, namely governmental and inter-governmental regulation, the role of trade unions and collective bargaining, as well as more critical forms of nongovernmental organization (NGO) activism and civil society protest."

The new business strategy on climate issues includes a strong dose of public relations, but it is not all hot air. Companies also have to demonstrate some tangible progress toward reducing emissions in order to blunt demands for more stringent regulation, and to protect their market positions in the event that mandatory emissions controls become a reality. While this strategy may sustain the political access and legitimacy of business, however, it is unlikely to result in the sustainable development that business now claims to champion. The IPCC report notes that greenhouse gases need to be slashed by more than 50% to stabilize the climate; the Kyoto Protocol called for a 5% cut in industrialized countries, and that target is fast becoming unreachable. There is still a long struggle ahead.

TWO CHEERS FOR OPEC

MARC BRESLOW

May/June 2000

So gasoline prices have risen above $1.50 a gallon and threaten to go even higher. To hear many commentators and politicians talk, this is a tragedy rivaling the bubonic plague of the Middle Ages. How dare OPEC threaten Americans' God-given right to cheap gas! Why, after all, did we fight the Gulf War and kill one hundred thousand Iraqis, if not to keep gas as cheap as bottled water?

No matter that even at $1.50 a gallon, gas is still not much more expensive, adjusted for inflation, than it was in the early 1970's, or that it is half the price that people pay in Britain, France, Germany, and Japan. It's still time to dip into the strategic oil reserve, cut the federal tax, and lift restrictions on oil drilling in environmentally-sensitive areas of Alaska.

I beg to differ. It's hard to think of another issue in which U.S. attitudes are more wrong-headed. The rest of the world knows that, because of global warming and because oil is eventually going to run out (unless we allow drilling to destroy every last bit of pristine environment anywhere), we have to reduce our burning of fossil fuels, including oil. Only the United States, under political domination of the oil and auto companies, refuses to recognize reality.

Higher gas prices are one of the best things that could happen to this country. If we are lucky, they will start a trend toward smaller cars and away from SUVs. In the long run SUVs threaten to destroy the global environment. In the short run, they threaten to kill all of us foolish—or cash poor—enough to continue driving normal cars. Federal regulators have found that in a collision between an SUV and a car, car occupants are three times as likely to be killed as if they were hit by another car.

Just recently automakers have finally acknowledged this fact, and say they will redesign future SUV models with lower frames to make them less of a threat. But wouldn't it make more sense to just get rid of most of them? Doubling gas prices would be the surest way of making that happen.

Won't that hurt the U.S. economy? Well, yes. Unfortunately, once you have built an economy on wasting energy, rebuilding it in an energy-efficient manner will involve substantial costs. And that is a reason to make the transition gradual—perhaps raising gas prices 20 cents a year for the next ten years would be reasonable schedule. By that time most people would be ready to get rid of their old gas guzzlers anyway. Not only could they downsize, but they could buy one of the new "hybrids," combination gas/electric vehicles (the engine charges the batteries) that Honda and Toyota are releasing this year. Just changing from SUVs (which get 15 or so miles to the gallon) to these hybrids (which get 60 or more), would go a long way toward meeting the United States' commitment to reduce carbon dioxide emissions in response to global warming.

What about the effects of higher fuel prices on moderate- and low-income people, who may be driving regular cars but still can't afford gas at $2 or $3 a gallon? There is an answer here. Rather than let the Kuwaiti royal family get the benefits of oil scarcity, we should do what Europe and Japan do—tax the hell out of oil (and coal and natural gas, which also create carbon dioxide when burned). Then we should redistribute the tax revenues in a progressive manner, so that low-income people come out even or ahead.

Peter Barnes, creator of the Sky Trust Initiative, has perhaps the best proposal for how to do this. He suggests that rather than letting the federal government use the oil-tax revenue on anything it wants—which could be something horribly regressive like further cuts in income or capital gains taxes—the money should go into a trust fund. Then it should be handed back to every U.S. resident on an equal per-capita basis. This method would mean low-income households getting back more than they pay for higher fuel costs—so we help the environment and economic equity at the same time. Not to mention sticking it to Exxon.

Resources: Earthday Network, <www.earthday.net>; the Sky Trust Initiative, <www.skytrust.org>; The union of Concerned Scientists, <www.ucsusa.org>; the Sierra Club, including its program on Transportation and Sprawl, <www.sierraclub.org>.

TOWARD A GLOBAL ENERGY TRANSITION

What would it take to reverse climate change?

ROSS GELBSPAN

March/April 2004

In 1998, Hurricane Mitch killed 10,000 people in Central America. Last May, the worst flooding in memory in Sri Lanka killed about 300 people, left another 500 missing, and left 350,000 homeless. The president of Tuvalu, an island nation in the Pacific threatened by rising sea levels, calls climate change "a form of slow death."

These are just a few recent natural disasters that scientists fear may be linked to global warming.

To avert climate catastrophe, humanity needs to cut its use of fossil fuels by at least 70% in a very short time. That is the consensus of more than 2,000 scientists from 100 countries reporting to the U.N.-sponsored Intergovernmental Panel on Climate Change in the largest and most rigorously peer-reviewed scientific collaboration in history.

The urgency of the threat is spelled out in two other recent peer-reviewed studies corroborating the U.N. panel's findings. The first, written in 2001 by researchers at the Hadley Center, Britain's principle climate research institute, estimated that the climate will change 50% more quickly than scientists had previously believed. Earlier computer models had assumed a relatively static biosphere. But when researchers factored in the warming that has already taken place, they found that the rate of change is compounding. They project that most of the world's forests will begin to die off and emit, rather than absorb, CO_2 by around 2040.

The other study is equally troubling. Several years ago, a team of 11 researchers published a study in Nature suggesting that unless the world gets half its energy from non-carbon (that is, non-fossil fuel) sources by 2018, a doubling—and possible tripling—of pre-industrial carbon dioxide (CO_2) levels later in this century will be inevitable. A follow-up study, published in Science in November 2002, calls for a crash program to develop a carbon-free energy economy. Using conservative projections of future energy use, the researchers concluded that within 50 years, the world will need to generate at least three times more energy from alternative sources than it currently produces from fossil fuels in order to avoid a catastrophic build-up of atmospheric CO_2.

The science is taken very seriously outside the United States. In other countries, hardly anyone debates whether human activities are affecting the climate. Policymakers in Europe are in agreement about the urgency of the climate threat. Holland has completed a plan to cut emissions by 80% in the next 40 years. The United Kingdom has committed itself to 60% reductions in 50 years. Germany is planning for 50% cuts in 50 years.

By contrast, the White House has become the East Coast branch office of Exxon-Mobil and Peabody Coal, and climate and energy policy has become the pre-eminent case study in the contamination of the U.S. political system by money.

Two years ago, U.S. President George W. Bush reneged on a campaign promise to cap carbon emissions from coal-burning power plants. He then unveiled his administration's energy plan, which is basically a shortcut to climate hell. (See "National Energy Plan?" p. 26.) In a truly Orwellian stroke, the White House excised all references to the dangers of climate change on the Environmental Protection Agency's website in mid-2003. Finally, Bush withdrew the United States from the Kyoto climate negotiations, and the administration's chief climate negotiator declared that the United States would not engage in the Kyoto process for at least 10 years.

A Strategy to Reverse CO_2 Emissions

A plan that could actually stabilize the climate does exist. Provisionally called the World Energy Modernization Plan, it was developed by an ad hoc group of about 15 economists, energy policy experts, and others who met at the Center for Health and the Global Environment at Harvard Medical School three years ago.

The plan addresses a stark reality: The deep oceans are warming, the tundra is thawing, the glaciers are melting, infectious diseases are migrating, and the timing of the seasons has changed. All this has resulted from only one degree of warming. The U.N.-sponsored Intergovernmental Panel on Climate Change (IPCC) expects the earth to warm another three to 10 degrees later in this century.

To date, no other policy proposals have adequately addressed either the scope or the urgency of the problem. While some of its particulars may require revamping, the World Energy Modernization Plan reflects an appropriate scale of action, given the magnitude of the crisis.

The plan calls for three interacting strategies. One is a subsidy switch: industrial countries would eliminate government subsidies for fossil fuels and establish equivalent subsidies for renewable, non-carbon energy technologies. Another is a clean-energy transfer fund—a pool of money on the order of $300 billion a year to provide renewable energy technologies to developing countries. The last element is a progressively more stringent fossil-fuel efficiency standard that would rise by 5% per year.

While each of these strategies can be viewed as a stand-alone reform, they are better understood as a set of interactive policies that could speed the energy transition far more rapidly together than if they were implemented piecemeal.

Subsidy Switch

The United States now spends more than $20 billion a year to subsidize fossil fuels through corporate tax write-offs and direct payments to oil, gas, and coal companies (for research and development, and oil purchases for the Strategic Petroleum Reserve, for example). Subsidies for fossil fuels in industrial countries total an estimated $200 billion a year.

Under this proposal, industrial countries would withdraw those subsidies from fossil fuels and establish equivalent subsidies for renewable energy sources. A small portion of U.S. subsidies must be used to retrain or buy out the nation's approximately 50,000 coal miners. But the lion's share of the subsidies would go to aggressive development of fuel cells, wind farms, and solar systems. The major oil companies would be forced to re-tool and retrain their workers to stay afloat in the renewable energy economy.

Fund to Help Poor Countries Go Green

The second element of the plan involves the creation of a new $300-billion-a-year fund to help transfer renewable energy technologies to the global South. Developing countries such as China, Mexico, Thailand, and Chile contain some of the world's smoggiest cities. Many would love to go solar, but virtually none can afford to.

One attractive source of revenue to fund the transfer lies in a so-called "Tobin tax," named after its developer, Nobel prize-winning economist James Tobin. This tax would be levied on banks and other agents that conduct international currency transactions. Tobin conceived his tax as a way of damping volatility in capital markets by discouraging short-term trading and encouraging longer-term capital investments. But it would also generate enormous revenues. Today currency swaps by banks and speculators total $1.5 trillion per day. A tax of a quarter-penny on a dollar would net $300 billion a year, which could go for wind farms in India, fuel-cell factories in South Africa, solar equipment assemblies in El Salvador, and vast, solar-powered hydrogen-producing farms in the Middle East.

If a Tobin tax proves unacceptable, a fund of the same magnitude could be raised from a tax on airline travel or a carbon tax in industrial countries, although both these sources are more regressive.

Regardless of its revenue source, the fund would be allocated according to a United Nations formula. Climate, energy use, population, economic growth rates, and other factors would determine each developing country's allocation.

Recipient countries would negotiate contracts with renewable energy vendors to ensure domestic ownership of new energy facilities and substantial employment of local labor in their construction and operation. Although not explicitly mentioned in the initial version of the plan, it would be important for governments to be required to include representatives of ethnic and indigenous minorities, universities, nongovernmental organizations (NGOs), and labor unions in making decisions about the procurement and deployment of new energy resources.

An international auditing agency would monitor transactions to ensure equal access for all energy vendors and to review contracting procedures between banks, vendors, and recipient governments.

Individual countries would decide how to use their share. For example, if India received $5 billion in the first year, it could pick its own mix of wind farms, small-scale solar installations, fuel cell generators, and biogas facilities.

In this hypothetical example, the Indian government would entertain bids for these clean energy projects. Vendors might include large or small private companies, state-owned entities, and even nonprofit organizations. As these contractors met specified development and construction goals, they would be paid directly by the banks. And the banks would receive fees for administering the fund.

As developing countries acquired technology, the fund could simply be phased out, or the money in it could be diverted to other global needs.

If funded by a Tobin tax, it would transfer resources from speculative, nonproductive finance-sector transactions to the industrial sectors of developing nations for productive, job-creating, wealth-generating projects. A clean-energy transfer fund of this sort could have a massive impact on developing and transitional economies, similar to the Marshall Plan's effect on Europe after World War II.

Strict International Efficiency Standards

Third, the plan calls on the parties to the Kyoto talks to adopt a simple and equitable fossil-fuel efficiency standard that becomes 5% more stringent each year.

This mechanism, if incorporated into the Kyoto Protocol, would harmonize and guide the global energy transition in a way that the current ineffectual and inequitable system of international emissions trading cannot.

The system of international emissions trading at the heart of the Kyoto Protocol is based on the concept that a country that exceeds its allowed quantity of carbon emissions can buy emission credits from a country that emits less than its allowed quantity. The United States, for instance, can pay Costa Rica to plant more trees to absorb carbon dioxide, and subtract the resulting reduction from its own allowance.

This system of international "cap and trade," as it is called in the jargon of the Kyoto negotiators, has significant failings: It's not enforceable and is plagued by irreconcilable equity disputes between the countries of the North and South. (See "Cap and Trade: Environmental Colonialism?")

International carbon trading cannot be the primary vehicle to propel a worldwide energy transition. Alone, it simply will not succeed in reversing—or even slowing—global CO_2 emissions at anywhere near an adequate rate. Even if all the problems with monitoring, enforcement, and equity could be resolved, emissions trading would at best be a fine-tuning instrument to help countries meet the final 10 to 15% of their obligation to reduce CO_2 emissions. We simply can't finesse nature with accounting tricks.

Instead, the parties to the Kyoto talks should increase their fossil-fuel energy efficiency by 5% every year until the global 70% reduction is attained. That means a country would either produce the same amount of goods as in the previous year with 5% less carbon fuel, or produce 5% more goods with the same amount of carbon fuel use as the previous year. During the first few years under the proposed efficiency standard, most countries would likely meet their goals by implementing low-cost

CAP AND TRADE: ENVIRONMENTAL COLONIALISM?

The global South has long contended that the Kyoto cap and trade system is unjust. Under Kyoto, each country's emissions cap is based on its 1990 emission levels—but developing countries argue that only a per-capita allocation of emission rights is fair. What's more, they argue, provisions in the Kyoto Protocol allow industrial nations to buy limitless amounts of cheap emission reductions in developing countries and to bank them indefinitely into the future. As the late Anil Agarwal, founder of the Centre for Science and Environment in New Delhi, has pointed out, when developing nations eventually become obligated to cut their own emissions (under a subsequent round of the Kyoto Protocol), they will be left with only the most expensive options. Agarwal considered this a form of environmental colonialism.

improvements to their existing energy systems. After a few years, however, more expensive technology would be required to meet the progressively higher standard, making renewable energy sources more cost effective in comparison to fossil-fuel efficiency measures. The growing demand would create mass markets and economies of scale for renewables.

Given both fossil-fuel efficiency improvements and the growing use of alternatives, emissions reductions would outpace long-term economic growth, benefiting the environment.

Every country would begin at its current baseline for emission levels, which would reduce the inequities inherent in the cap-and-trade system.

This approach would be far simpler to negotiate than the current protocol, with its morass of emissions trading details, reviews of the adequacy of commitments, and differentiated emission targets for each country. It would also be easier to monitor and enforce. A nation's compliance would be measured simply by calculating the annual change in the ratio of its carbon fuel use to its gross domestic product. That ratio would have to change by 5% a year. Although this plan does not include an enforcement mechanism, one would be devised.

The approach has a precedent in the Montreal Protocol, under which companies phased out ozone-destroying chemicals. That protocol was successful because the companies that made the destructive chemicals were able to produce their substitutes with no loss of competitive standing within the industry. The energy industry must be restructured in the same way. Several oil executives have said in private conversations that they could, in an orderly fashion, decarbonize their energy supplies—but only if the governments of the world regulate the process to require all companies to make the transition in lockstep. A progressive fossil-fuel efficiency standard would provide that type of regulation.

A Regulated Transition

Even from the perspective of capitalist financial institutions, this plan should make perfect sense. Recently, Swiss Re-Insurance said it anticipates losses from climate impacts to reach $150 billion a year within this decade. Munich Re, the world's largest reinsurer, estimates that within several decades, losses from climate impacts will reach $300 billion a year. Climate change will destroy property; raise health care costs; ruin crops; and damage energy, communications and transportation infrastructures. It will likely wound the insurance and banking sectors in the process. Last year, the largest re-insurer in Britain said that unchecked climate change could bankrupt the global economy by 2065. And its effects hit poor countries hardest—not because nature discriminates against the poor, but because poor countries can't afford the kinds of infrastructure needed to buffer its impacts.

By contrast, a worldwide energy transition would create a dramatic expansion of the overall wealth in the global economy. It would raise living standards in the South without compromising those in the North. Rewiring the planet with clean energy in time to meet nature's deadline will generate a staggering number of new jobs for the global labor force. By blocking a transition to clean energy, the coal and oil industries are hindering a huge surge in new jobs all over the world.

This transition cannot be accomplished by unregulated free markets. A global energy conversion will require the world's governments to put in place a strong regime of mandatory regulation to control the economic activity of some of the world's largest and most powerful corporations. Without a binding structure of regulation to level the corporate playing field, competing energy companies will undercut today's voluntary initiatives by selling artificially cheaper oil and coal products. This would turn any investment in solar, wind, and hydrogen into money losers. On the other hand, energy firms that submit to the strong new regulations would gain a new $300-billion-a-year market.

A meaningful solution to the climate crisis could potentially be the beginning of a much larger transformation of our social and economic dynamics. This proposal is ambitious. But the alternative—given the escalating instability of the climate system and the increasing desperation caused by global economic inequities—is truly too horrible to contemplate.

Adapted with permission from Foreign Policy In Focus (FPIF) <www. fpif.org>, a joint project of the Interhemispheric Resource Center and the Institute for Policy Studies. A longer version of this article was prepared for the PetroPolitics conference co-sponsored by FPIP and the Sustainable Energy and Economy Network (SEEN), a project of the Institute for Policy Studies. For more information, and to read the web version of the article online, see <www.PetroPolitics.org>.

NATIONAL ENERGY PLAN?

ADRIA SCHARF AND THAD WILLIAMSON

March/April 2004

One huge political obstacle stands in the way of weaning the U.S. economy from fossil fuels: the all-but-certain opposition of leading energy corporations and other industries with vested interests in the status quo. Corporate interests have aggressively attacked environmentalists (starting with Rachel Carson) and environmental legislation at every turn over the past five decades, their opposition all too often proving deadly to even modest environmental reform proposals. (See "Industry Attacks on Dissent," in Chapter 2.)

During the current Bush administration, large corporate interests have gone from simply influencing energy-related policies to literally making them. Within days of taking office, George W. Bush appointed the National Energy Policy Development Group (NEPD), a task force headed by Vice President Dick Cheney, with the mandate to define the nation's energy policy for the new century. With the former CEO of the oil-services firm Halliburton at its helm, the task force consulted in secret with the captains of the nation's oil, nuclear, and coal industries, refusing to this day to name the meeting attendees or release minutes from the talks. The group issued its recommendations in May 2001. Its "National Energy Plan" takes as a given that over the next 20 years, U.S. oil consumption will increase by 33%, natural gas consumption by well over 50%, and demand for electricity by 45%. Rather than lay out a strategy to reduce the country's rapacious appetite for fossil fuels, the report focuses on how to feed the beast, making no real attempt to reduce aggregate fossil-fuel consumption, seriously raise energy efficiency, or aggressively build non-carbon alternatives (other than nuclear energy). In fact, the plan makes virtually no mention of promising forms of alternative energy like wind power.

Instead, it proposes the United States acquire more energy by drilling in the Arctic National Wildlife Refuge (ANWR) and offshore areas, building new electricity plants, burning more coal, and by continuing to import petroleum, both from our current suppliers—Saudi Arabia, Canada, Mexico, Venezuela—and, increasingly, from countries in the Caucasus, Central Asia, and Africa. The report recommends repeatedly that defense and trade policy be structured to ensure U.S. access to new oil supplies—and to commercial opportunities in the energy sector—in these regions.

"Big energy companies all but held the pencil for the White House task force as government officials wrote a plan calling for billions of dollars in corporate subsidies, and the wholesale elimination of key health and environmental safeguards," according to Natural Resources Defense Council (NRDC) president John H. Adams. The NRDC, which forced the Department of Energy to release some task-force documents by court order, concluded that oil industry representatives essentially wrote whole sections of the national energy policy. Bush's "Executive Order 13211," which requires government agencies to prepare "statements of energy effects" before implementing any policy that might affect energy supply, distribution, or use, was "nearly identical in structure and impact to [an American Petroleum Institute] draft, and nearly verbatim in a key section." A Bush proposal to weaken the Clean Air Act originated from a lobbyist for the electricity firm Southern Company, a major Bush donor.

Senate Democrats staved off ANWR drilling in 2003 by threatening to filibuster. But Bush has accomplished other key plan recommendations—including the expansion of drilling in Alaska's ecologically sensitive, federally managed outer continental shelf—through executive orders. Senate Republicans aim to pass the major remaining components of the legislation as stand-alone bills and amendments this session.

The political obstacles to major climate-change reform transcend the particulars of any single administration. Al Gore's attempts to pass a modest carbon tax are instructive. Long an advocate of taxing fossil fuels, Gore tried and failed to pass a carbon tax in the Senate in 1991. One of the first initiatives put forward by the new Clinton-Gore administration in 1993 was a small tax on fossil fuels, called a BTU tax, meant to force down fossil-fuel consumption and generate revenue. Despite

Gore's strong support, the $73 billion five-year tax proposal was quickly trampled by both parties. Democrats and Republicans alike simply did not, and do not, see the tax as politically palatable. By 1998, in public statements about the Kyoto Protocol, a chastened Al Gore assured the legislature, and the oil and auto lobbies, that no carbon tax would be used to lower carbon emissions under the Kyoto accord. Gore said the administration had "completely ruled out new taxes of any kind as a means of meeting our obligations."

In short, there is a mismatch between the dramatic changes in our energy use needed if climate change is to be addressed rationally, and the capacity of the existing political-economic system to deliver such change. Environmentalists and others who are serious about achieving real policy change to address the global-warming threat must be equally serious about forthrightly challenging the power structures that make sane environmental policies all but impossible to achieve.

Resources: Natural Resources Defense Council <www.nrdc.org>; Report of the National Energy Policy Development Group <www.whitehouse.gov/energy>.

CHAPTER 4

GLOBAL CAPITALISM AND RESOURCES SCARCITY

WRINGING OUT THE WORLD

LAURA ORLANDO

July/August 1999

Water as an environmental topic is a bit like climate change. Until you reach for your winter coat on a gray August day in New York City, you will not believe things are as bad as they say. Same goes with water. When you turn on the spigot and hear the pipes clank but see no water, only then will your concern be palpable.

A conservative estimate of the number of people living in countries with "absolute water scarcity" by 2025 is one billion. Countries like China, India, Mexico and South Africa do not have sufficient water resources to meet reasonable per capita water needs for their rapidly expanding populations. Water scarcity means women spend more of their time finding and carrying water, farmers lose their land, infant mortality climbs, and public health suffers. And as the stakes get higher, it may mean war.

Globally, fresh water is abundant; it just is not always accessible to households, industry, or farmers. Where it is accessible, it is either being polluted or drawn down to shockingly depleted reservoirs. Agriculture accounts for two-thirds of global water use. Most of the water used in agriculture comes from either rivers or groundwater wells and is used to irrigate crops. Every year, humans draw from these sources the equivalent of five times the annual flow of the Mississippi River for use on 16% of the world's cropland and ever year there is less water to tap.

Ecologically, human-induced water scarcity is a death knell for biodiversity. In southeastern Arizona, Sierra Vista and neighboring communities along the San Pedro River are pumping so much water from the aquifer that supplies the river it is expected that parts of the San Pedro will be dry within the next ten years. As a refuge in the Sonoran desert for four million migratory birds heading south before the North American winter sets in, the San Pedro's demise will devastate bird populations. There is no place else for them to go in this desert country except to the grave.

Water scarcity leads to declining water quality and pollution and has an especially adverse impact on poor people. Rural economies usually bow to the needs of cities and so when the availability of water gets tight, we can expect rural (read "small") farmers to lose their water so that city-dwellers can flush their toilets and run their factories.

Disease and death climb as water quality and quantity decline. The United Nations International Children's Emergency Fund (UNICEF) reports that 40,000 children worldwide are dying daily from hunger or disease caused by lack of water or contaminated water. Keep in mind, 40,000 children are dying every day before the predicted water scarcity problems climax. Forty per cent of people living in Africa are already at risk of death or disease from water scarcity or contamination. The kind of food poor people eat also is affected by the availability of water. People below the poverty line in Asia spend approximately 60% of their total income on cereals (which provide over 72% of their total nutrients). It has been estimated that over 80% of the total increase in cereal production in Asia since the 1960s has been from irrigated land. What will they eat when the water that feeds the green revolution dries up?

Water, like money, flows to the rich. And water, like borders, will increasingly start wars. In the mid-1980s, U.S. government intelligence services estimated that there were at least ten places in the world where war could break out over shared water resources. The situation is only getting worse in places like the Middle East and North Africa. Ethiopia controls 80% of the Nile's flow, yet almost the entire population of Egypt depends on its water. Nearly all of Egypt's cropland is irrigated yet no formal protocol exists among Nile River riparians for sharing its flow. Turkey controls the headwaters of the Tigris and Euphrates. Iraq and Syria are downstream. In 1983, Turkey initiated the South East Anatolia Development Project, known by its Turkish acronym GAP. When completed, the project will consist of 21 dams, including the massive Ataturk Dam, and cost over US$21 billion. When Turkey filled the gigantic reservoir of the Ataturk Dam in 1990, they completely stopped the flow of the Euphrates for one month. Iraq and Syria are outraged by Turkey's water hoarding. Syria's support for the Marxist Kurdish Party (PKK), which is waging an independence campaign against the Turkish government, has no small part in its escalating water disputes with Turkey.

Big dams and diversion canals are the workhorses of modern irrigation schemes. The water they deliver is heavily subsidized by government and flows first to large landowners. It follows the same logic as trickle down capitalism, and like its brethren, leaves a trickle that hardly parches a poor man's thirst let alone waters his crops. Irrigation isn't cheap. It costs between $1,500 and $10,000 per hectare, depending on where and how the water is being delivered. The World Bank has provided the greatest single source of funds for large dam construction with US$50 billion (1992 dollars) for construction of more than 500 large dams (large in this context means taller than a four-story building). Dams are not environmentally friendly, no matter how much ballyhoo you hear about "clean" hydropower or flood control. A 1990 internal survey of World Bank hydroelectric dam projects (dams are often multipurpose, so hydroelectric dams often provide irrigation water) showed that 58% were planned and built without any consideration of downstream impacts that would cause massive coastal erosion, pollution and other problems.

Irrigation brings with it mounting problems; such as waterlogged and salinized soils, shrinking and contaminated aquifers, the destruction of aquatic habitat, and large refugee populations pushed off their land by dams—like the 1.3 million being displaced by China's disastrous Three Gorges Dam on the Yangtze River. Increasing water needs and degraded environmental conditions, coupled with the fact that the average efficiency of the irrigation systems used in the world today is a dismal 40%, has put the examination of modern irrigation front and center. Many people believe the appropriate course of action is to use water in agriculture more productively. Some go as far as to bring poverty and ecology issues to the table, a much needed but surprising orientation from the researchers, policymakers, and bankers that replaced "culture" in agriculture with "business." Things must be bad.

Since irrigation uses the lion's share of global water resources, it is the portal of conservation or ruination. In her new book *Pillar of Sand*, Sandra Postel warns that "time is of the essence." Postel is Director of the Global Water Policy Project in Amherst, Massachusetts. A veteran water watcher, she can hear the clock ticking when the rest of us hear only the sweet sound of a spring rain. Postel counsels that, "We need to double water productivity—get twice as much benefit from each liter of water we remove from rivers, lakes, and underground aquifers—if we are to have any hope of fulfilling the water requirements of eight billion people and protecting the natural ecosystems on which economies and life itself depend." Irrigation, she says, must become "leaner and smarter." Finding solutions with farmers rather than with engineers is a place to start. It means rolling up one's pant legs and stepping into the rice field to talk to farmers.

Moving from large, public irrigation projects to more flexible, knowledge-based, small scale efforts is a critical step in making irrigation more efficient, says Postel. Everyone involved, from finance to harvest, has a role in the transition. Access to credit, markets, and information will decide cultivation methods, crops and scale. Opening that access is the role of politics and policymakers. Reducing water lost to evaporation and seepage, capturing more fresh water before it flows into salt sinks, using salt resistant and less thirsty crops, improving soil conditions, and designing efficient irrigation systems, must involve not only engineers and scientists, but also farmers and rural communities. The consumer's job is to consume less grain-intensive and more water efficient food. Pork, for instance, will not be on the menu.

Even so, in 25 years we may be identifying countries not as "developed" or "less-developed," but as "upstream" or downstream" countries. "Water rich" will soon carry more cachet and economic clout that "oil rich." But before we change the text in the political science books and hunker down for the 21st century's water wars, we can do something about the water scarcity and flaring tempers. The first step is to acknowledge that clean water is more than a commodity resource. It is a fundamental component to human and ecological health. When push comes to shove, water's role in commerce—its use in industry and agriculture—must bow to meeting people's basic needs and maintaining ecological integrity. Environmental devastation, it should be remembered, is a serious public health problem. Water wars can be avoided with a resource management strategy based on preventive diplomacy, both at local and national levels, implemented in tandem with enforceable water agreements.

Since water recognizes no borders, these agreements should be linked treaties with regional and international mechanisms to enforce them. We should also consider implementing an international code of conduct for water use. The code of conduct would not only carry with it rules, but practical technical and management alternatives to address the water crisis and international financing to back up its recommendations. The world cannot afford to wait to hear the clank of the empty pipe before shifting gears to conserve, protect, and better distribute its fresh water resources.

Resources: Sandra Postel, *Pillar of Sand* (W.W. Norton and Company, 1999); Peter Gleick, *Water in Crisis* (Oxford University Press 1993); Robert S. Devine, "The Trouble With Dams," *Atlantic Monthly* (August 1995); Joyce R. Starr, "Water Wars," *Foreign Policy* (Spring 1982); International Rivers Network, 1847 Berkeley Way, Berkeley, CA 94703, 510-848-1155; 510-8481008 (fax), irnweb@irn.org, <www.irn.org>.

WHOSE RIGHT TO WATER?

Corporate water giants seek to privatize this most basic of all natural resources. Consumers and communities are fighting back.

KEVIN MURRAY

November/December 2003

> "[Water is] one of the world's great business opportunities. It promises to be to the 21st century what oil was to the 20th."
>
> —*Fortune*, May 2000

Arriving in Haiti by air provides a dramatic visual introduction to a country facing a long-term problem with water. From the sky, a few lush patches of green stand out against dry hillsides totally devoid of vegetation. The Haiti-Dominican Republic border appears as a sharp line where forest cover ends abruptly—on the Dominican side of the frontier.

Haiti receives enough rain that floods are common. But climate change is slowly changing rainfall patterns, and poor resource management policies mean that most of the rain that does fall rushes quickly back to the sea, taking with it large amounts of precious topsoil.

Topsoil erosion and deforestation have combined to put tremendous pressure on small-scale agriculture, still the only source of livelihood for millions of Haitians. Manielus Exil and his fellow members at the Kopa Koton agricultural cooperative face this pressure every day. But through learning and experimentation, they have slowly improved their management of local water and soil resources. For example, they have invested in a system that allows them to store water from a source located in the hills above their farmland. They use gravity to irrigate their crops in the dry season and have terraced their land to protect it from erosion during the rainy season. Now they are investigating the potential benefits of installing a drip irrigation system. They have established a tree nursery where they cultivate and then plant hundreds of saplings a year to reverse deforestation.

Still, the cooperative's members continue to live at the very margin of economic viability. By mid-2003, lack of rain threatened to push them over that edge. "We haven't seen hardly any rain for two years," explains Manielus. "Now the spring has almost dried up. No one remembers that ever happening before. Our water problem is getting worse." The cooperative faced catastrophic crop losses that would mean economic ruin and hunger bordering on starvation for co-op members and their families. What little food they had been able to store had long since been eaten.

Early-season rains did come to Papaye this year in amounts that allowed Kopa Koton and most of its neighbors to salvage some of their production. While they will be happy to have a harvest, cooperative members are under no illusion that their water problem has been solved.

Manielus Exil and his neighbors are not alone. One could tell a parallel story about the water woes of township dwellers in South Africa who face a cholera epidemic because they can no longer afford to pay for clean water. Local water authorities, under pressure from the World Bank to recover their costs, began metering water and hiked the price. In both rural and urban areas, chronic water shortage is a way of life for an increasing percentage of the world's population.

Why is this the case? We are using this resource much faster than it can be renewed, pumping aquifers dry in the process. The United Nations forecasts that, at current rates of population growth and water use, the per capita supply of usable fresh water will drop by one-third over the next 20 years. Even conservative projections suggest that one-third of the world's population will face serious water shortages by 2025.

The overall supply of water is not the only issue. Like most resources, water is unequally distributed within and among countries, making water equity an important issue. Part of this distribution problem is the "natural" result of population levels, climate, and ecological factors, but much of it reflects power relations and policy choices at national and international levels. Around the world, one in five people (1.1 billion) lack access to safe drinking water and over half (2.9 billion) lack adequate sanitation facilities—many in countries where national water supply is not a serious problem. Without safe water, people drink to their own death and disease. Each year there are 250 million new cases of water-related disease—mostly cholera and dysentery—and 10 million people die from those diseases.

Beyond drinking water, the world's water crisis is undermining millions of small-scale farmers across the globe. Agriculture accounts for 70% of world water use, but large-scale, corporate agriculture swallows up most of that water. As aquifers are pumped dry and water is diverted for commercial purposes, water tables fall and small farmers in many regions are finding it increasingly difficult to sustain their harvests.

The Global Challenge, the Market Response

No one disputes the fact that our unsustainable use of water has created a global water crisis of overuse, pollution, waste, and lack of access. A widely shared sense of crisis opens up the possibility of real change, and the international community has taken some important steps. However, privatization of water resources threatens to exacerbate the problem and throw millions more people into the ranks of the "water-poor."

At major international summits in 2000 and 2002, nations committed themselves to cutting the number of people without access to safe water or sanitation in half by 2015. Meeting these goals will require providing new water hookups for 300,000 people every year and new sanitation facilities for 400,000 per year. But most public water authorities are hard pressed to maintain existing services, let alone expand.

Enter Suez, Vivendi, Thames Water, and a small number of other corporations that have burst onto the global water scene over the past decade. These water giants offer to build large-scale water infrastructure in return for increased corporate involvement in the provision of water services via "public-private partnerships," a.k.a. water privatization. The private for-profit water industry has grown explosively over the past decade. Vivendi alone already supplies water to 110 million people. In 1990, private water companies operated in 12 countries; today they are in nearly 100. And industry analysts expect the private drinking water market to grow from its current level of about $500 billion to about $3 trillion in just the next five years.

The corporations typically sign long-term (25 to 30 year) contracts with a municipal or regional water authority that cedes to the corporation complete control over the water supply in question. The company sets rates and makes all investment decisions. Many contracts guarantee the private provider a minimum rate of return on investment, regardless of the quality of service. These contracts transfer control over a local or regional water supply to a single private company that is much more accountable to its shareholders than it is to any public entity or to water consumers.

The collapse of a public authority may drive the privatization process, but conditions placed on water loans by lenders like the World Bank have also played a key role. The Bank used to help countries build public water utilities, but, in a recent three-year period, 60% of Bank loans for water infrastructure carried conditions related to privatization. To date, most privatizations have occurred in Africa, Asia, and Latin America, but all of the water giants are now targeting Europe and the United States as priority areas for expansion.

The International Center for Investigative Journalism conducted an in-depth study of the track record of the water corporations and found that while privatization has improved service in some cases, "they [the companies] can be ruthless players who constantly push for higher rate increases, frequently fail to meet their commitments and abandon waterworks if they are not making enough money." For example, some residents of metro Manila greeted privatization as a miracle when two water companies were handed control over the city's water supply in 1997. Five years later, corruption charges, poor service, and the near collapse of one of the companies left the miracle more than a little tarnished. Suez pulled out of a celebrated agreement with the city of Buenos Aires, Argentina, when general economic collapse meant the company's profits did not meet expectations. And the city of Atlanta, Georgia, recently voted to cancel its $500 million contract with Suez's U.S. subsidiary, United Water, after widespread public complaints about poor service, declining water quality, and high user fees.

Privatization boosters point to a modest list of examples where water privatization has shown positive results. But they typically falter when asked to explain how privatization is going to bring water to the hundreds of millions of people who currently do not have access to it. Speaking to the Canadian Broadcasting Company, Gerard Payen, the architect of Suez's international expansion program, explained, "Water as a business is very effective when you look at the needs. We purify water and bring this water to your home. We provide a service, it has a cost, and somebody has to pay for it." Then how will the market bring water to people who can never afford to pay for it?

Privatization turns water, an essential common good, into a commodity like any other, to be owned, shifted across borders, and sold in search of the highest profit. For the corporate "water elites," water fits neatly into a vision of corporate-led global economic integration—along with sneakers, corn flakes, intellectual property rights, and the genetic material on which life is based. Water elites are often criticized for failing to recognize access to safe water as a right. But they clearly do have a rights-based perspective. Water corporations and their allies place a high priority on the establishment and protection of the unfettered right of corporations to own and trade the world's water as they see fit.

The Real Rights Solution

A growing network of social movements, community groups, and nongovernmental organizations supports a different notion of the right to water. National and cross-border networks like the Water for All Campaign, the Blue Planet Project, and the People's World Water Forum share with the water establishment a sense of urgency about water, but reject the notion that water is just another commodity or service. Instead, they consider it a fundamental human right. They share the water establishment's interest in conservation and limiting water waste, but question its reliance on large infrastructure projects, especially dams, and on water privatization.

The new water activists recognize the limitations of many public water authorities. Clearly, some water authorities are inefficient bureaucracies that politicians use to reward relatives and supporters. Even where water authorities are committed to providing water to all, public disinvestment and the "hollowing out" of the state over the past two decades have made their job very difficult. A massive public investment program is part of the solution to the water crisis; redirecting the subsidies and investment capital now flowing to private corporations would provide a good start.

Money alone, however, will not solve the water crisis. Public water authorities are going to have to become much more creative and democratic, finding new ways to turn water "customers" into active participants in the development of water policy. There are already plenty of examples of public water authorities—Porto Alegre, Brazil, and Bogota, Colombia, for example—that have built successful programs encouraging public involvement in campaigns against water waste and in the implementation of new technologies.

In many rural areas, water activists favor decentralized, community-based resource management, supported but not dominated by public authorities. Farmers all over the world are joining those of Haiti's Central Plateau in taking steps to become more effective stewards of water resources. Too often, those farmers end up facing the opposition of public water or power authorities interested in developing a dam or other large infrastructure project, or in giving a private corporation control over local resources. In a new vision of "public-public partnership," activists advocate public support for community-based watershed management rather than the handoff of public water resources to private, for-profit corporations.

Adherents to radically different views of how to solve the water crisis are working to put their visions into practice in urban and rural communities all around the world. In some cases, the result has been creative solutions to local water challenges. In many others, local groups have challenged and blocked plans to increase private control over the water supply. For example:

- In Mecosta County, Michigan, a determined citizen coalition has opposed the efforts of a bottled water subsidiary of the Nestle corporation to gain private control of important groundwater supplies. In 2001, the county licensed the company (then a Perrier subsidiary) to open a bottling plant in Stanwood, Michigan, for a fee of less than $100 a year. Almost before anyone knew about it, the company was pumping a half million gallons of water a day from an aquifer beneath a hunting reserve. After learning about the plan, Michigan Citizens for Water Conservation launched a direct action campaign against Nestle and sought a temporary injunction to stop the pumps while the court decided on the legality of Nestle's use of the water. The injunction has yet to be granted.

- In Cochabamba, Bolivia, violent conflict broke out in 1999, when a Bechtel subsidiary signed a 40-year contract to operate municipal water services there. The private operator dramatically raised water fees during the first year. Well-organized public resistance led the municipality to rescind the contract with Bechtel, but the corporation sued Cochabamba for damages before a secret World Bank panel. The water is back in public hands, but the public authority still faces the same daunting challenges it faced before its flirtation with privatization. Plans exist to upgrade water services and extend them to more residents, but it is unclear where the authority will get the necessary $200 million.
- In many locations, governments, power companies, and irrigation interests have promoted the construction of large-scale dams in response to water and electricity problems. Dams often flood out thousands of local residents and completely destroy regional watershed systems, but they continue to get political support because they supply electricity to power-hungry urban areas and facilitate large-scale irrigation projects supporting corporate agriculture. In August 2003, activists from the Brazilian Movement of Dam-Affected People (MAB) occupied dams throughout Brazil. Among other things, MAB was demanding reparations for Brazilians whose lives have been destroyed by dam projects.

Kyoto Blues

In March 2003, 24,000 government and U.N. officials, civil society activists, corporate executives, journalists, and water specialists gathered in Kyoto, Japan, for the third World Water Forum. Organized by the Marseilles-based World Water Council (WWC), the forum quickly became a stage for debate over the water crisis and potential solutions.

It was "asymmetrical warfare," given the enormous resources at the disposal of corporate representatives and their control over the forum agenda. Those promoting the notion of a universal right to water did, however, get their voices heard. Freely referring to corporate water giants by name, activists charged that the forum had become a public relations event promoting a corporate view of the water crisis. The anti-dam International Rivers Network insisted that the forum was controlled by a "mafia" of irrigation- and power-agency representatives in tandem with the water multinationals. The forum may pose as a search for solutions to benefit the world's poor, but, according to an IRN representative, "in reality, their pseudo-solutions are driven by personal, institutional, corporate, and political interests."

A look at the composition of the WWC lends credence to the charge of elite control. The organization is led by Egypt's Minister of Water Resources and Irrigation. Its vice presidents include a Suez executive and a former vice president of the World Bank, and its Board of Governors is an elite club of power players in the world of dams, irrigation, hydropower, and water privatization.

To no one's surprise, the forum's final Ministerial Declaration failed to commit governments to review individual dam projects. It also quite consciously declined to recognize a universal human right to water. Activists did claim a victory in the forum's decision to declare that the results of water privatization have been mixed and that "the debate concerning public-private partnerships has not been resolved."

This last issue is extremely important to the corporations. They seem willing to invest some of their own money in water privatization projects in the developed countries, where users can pay fees that guarantee sufficient profits. In the global South, however, higher risk and lower rates of return mean that the water giants require massive public financing to make privatization work. Whether the World Bank and other international financial institutions continue to promote the current "public-private partnership" model will thus play a critical role in the outcome of the new water wars.

Toward a New Social Contract on Water

While the World Water Forum met in Japan, water activists held alternative gatherings in Florence, New Delhi, New York, and São Paulo to protest the approach being taken in Kyoto and to promote the notion that water is a human right and a common resource.

Activists are committed to creating a vision that moves beyond opposing dam construction and blocking water privatization to develop principles for a sustainable global water system and concrete proposals to bring that system into existence. They continue down the challenging path of integrating the vision of Haitian farmers struggling for community control of water with that of Michigan environmental activists fighting to keep public water out of the hands of bottled water companies. In September 2003, many members of this network were in Cancún, working to keep water out of the World Trade Organization's agreement on services. The end of this debate is not in sight.

In 1998, an international group of politicians, academics, and NGO leaders formed the Committee for a World Water Contract. Their *World Water Manifesto* opens with a challenge:

> 1.4 billion of the planet's 5.8 billion inhabitants do not have access to drinking water, the fundamental source of life. This fact is intolerable. Now, the risk is great that in the year 2020 when the world population reaches around 8 billion human beings, the number of people without access to drinking water will increase to more than 3 billion. This is unacceptable. We can and must prevent the unacceptable becoming possible. How?

The committee points to the recognition of a universal right to water, the need for a massive global educational campaign on the water crisis, and the creation of citizen "water parliaments" to address water issues. For their part, the new corporate water giants plan to continue turning water into a profitable commodity—"blue gold." The water wars have just begun.

Resources: Maude Barlow and Tony Clarke, *Blue Gold* (New Press, 2002); International Center for Investigative Journalism, "The Water Barons: A Handful of Corporations Seek to Privatize the World's Water" (Feb. 2003) <www.icij.org/water>; Leah C. Wells, "In Iraq, Water and Oil Do Mix," ***Counterpunch*** 5/16/03; Vandana Shiva, "Bechtel and Blood for Water," *Z-Net* 5/12/03.

HUNTERS OR SHEPHERDS OF THE SEA?
UNDERSTANDING THE FISHERIES CRISIS OF THE NORTHWEST ATLANTIC

SAMUEL SCOTT

January/February 2001

On October 29, 2000, the Portland, Maine, fishing community gathered on the city's Fish Pier to hold a memorial service for Carlyle "Butch" Minot. Minot's body had been recovered four days earlier, 35 miles off the coast. Caught between declining catches and restrictions on the amount of time that can be spent at sea, fishers are accepting greater risks in an already dangerous industry. Minot, the fifth member of the Portland fishing community lost at sea in the year 2000, had been fishing by himself when he was lost. Another fisher said of Minot's decision to go out alone, "It's stupid. It shouldn't be done. I've done it myself and it's stupid." In coastal communities throughout the northeast United States and Atlantic Canada, however, fishers face a crushing dilemma of working harder and at greater risk than ever before, or getting out of the life altogether.

Throughout the 500-year history of commercial fishing in the northwest Atlantic, there has been one constant: the fishers harvesting the sea have worked at the limits of their ships, their gear, and their bodies. At a high cost in both lives and vessels, they have worked hard to catch as many fish as they could, as fast as they could, and for as long as they could. In the process, they have created an industrial culture that emphasizes working at high risk to maximize the catch. The introduction over the last half century of new technologies in fishing, food processing, and food distribution has created an unbearable burden on the ecosystems of the northwest Atlantic. The crisis will require a fundamental shift not only in how fisheries are managed, but also in how the peoples and communities living along the shores of this region understand their relationship to the sea.

To the Limit

While the fishers of the 19th century, like their present-day counterparts, pushed themselves and their equipment as far as they could, their maximum catch remained well within the sustainable limits of the northwest Atlantic ecosystem. The fishing grounds were so productive, in fact, that contemporary experts predicted that they could never be exhausted. As long as the fishers worked from sailing vessels with hook and line, these predictions might have held true. However, two crucial developments, occurring on either side of the turn of the 20th century, destroyed the balance: the introduction of the steel-hulled fishing trawler and the perfection of refrigeration and frozen foods.

The change in vessel in the late 19th century allowed for a entirely new method of catching fish. The net replaced the hook and line as the primary method of capture. The new boats could drag an enormous sack-shaped net across the ocean bottom where the most highly prized species of fish lived. This method was called trawling, and the word trawler soon became synonymous with fishing boat throughout the North Atlantic. Trawlers immediately began landing catches six times greater than the fishing schooners. The fishers, used to driving both themselves and their vessels to the breaking point, now had a vessel whose endurance and durability were far greater than before. Fishers from the United States and Canada were joined in their traditional waters by Europeans—English, French, and Spanish—who used the speed and endurance of the new trawlers to extend their scope far west from Europe.

The unprecedented catches were fed into a market radically enlarged by the introduction of frozen-food technology in the early decades of the 20th century. The emergence of distribution centers like the large fish markets in Boston and New York were a boon to seafood processors. Focused distribution allowed them to control most of the catch without needing to invest directly in fishing vessels and crews. Freezing and fast transportation allowed them to extend the market for fresh fish to consumers living far from the smell of salt air. As a result, fishers had every economic incentive to use their new vessels to their fullest extent.

Below the waters, however, the marvelous fishing grounds that had supported centuries of intensive harvesting were beginning to change. As the vast amounts of fish being harvested began to strain the fish population, the method of capture was damaging the ecosystem's ability to recover. The bottom-dragging trawls that could sweep tons of fish from the ocean floor also caused significant damage to the fishes' habitat. It did not take long for the double stress of overfishing and habitat destruction to cause noticeable declines in the catch. The fishers responded with the customary aggressiveness. More powerful vessels and more efficient gear were employed by fishers working ever harder to sustain the catch levels they had come to expect. The fishers were whipped into an even greater sense of urgency by the intense competition among the multinational fleets present on the fishing grounds. The predictable result was an accelerated degradation of the ecosystem.

By the 1960s the inability of the northwest Atlantic ecosystem to sustain the level of harvest was undeniable. The response by the fishing nations was one of national protectionism. The extension of national sovereignty over vast expanses of ocean took some time to emerge, but by the mid-1970s most nations had laid claim to exclusive fishing rights up to 200 miles from their shores. The lucrative fishing grounds of the northwest Atlantic largely fell to the United States and Canada, and their respective fishing fleets immediately reaped the benefits. So great was the prize of the grounds that the two nations could not agree where the demarcation line between the two zones fell. An international court arbitrated nearly a decade later. The resulting Hague Line, established in 1984, pleased no one, and has been a source of contention ever since, particularly because the line bisects George's Bank, one of the region's richest grounds.

The 200-mile limits, and the resulting departure of the international fleets from their waters, brought good days for the U.S. and Canadian fishing industries. This windfall only served to reinforce an industrial culture that pushed body and boat to the limit. It took very little time for the domestic fishing fleets to make up for the capacity of the departed foreign fleets. In fact, they soon both outstripped the industry's prior harvest capacity and brought the total catch to unprecedented levels. By the end of the 1980s the assault on the fish populations finally reached catastrophic proportions and the fish stocks began to collapse.

The fishing communities bore the economic brunt of the ecological crisis. Unemployment in Gloucester and New Bedford, two of the largest fishing ports in Massachusetts, for example, consistently exceeds the statewide rate—sometimes by nearly double. Traditional structures of credit, whereby fishers could fuel, provision, and maintain their vessels based on the return of future voyages, are deteriorating and disappearing throughout the Massachusetts fishing ports. In 1994, Gloucester's fishing population numbered around 400, down from 2,000 at mid-century. In the same year, the National Marine Fisheries Service estimated that the Gloucester fishing fleet was twice as large as the current fish stocks could sustain. In the year 2000, a report to the New England Fishery Management Council concluded that fish populations were well below the targets necessary for rebuilding stocks and recommended further reductions in both the overall fishing effort and the fleet capacity.

Too Little, Too Late

Faced with the protests of the fishing communities and criticism from environmentalists, the Canadian and U.S. governments tried various belated strategies to shore up the plummeting fish populations. In the aftermath of the 200-mile limits, the Canadian government promoted the integration of the fishing industry as part of an economic- development package for the depressed Atlantic provinces. It fostered local fish-processing facilities that owned their own fleets of trawlers. Ultimately, these large concerns came to own almost half of the Canadian fleet capacity. Canadian regulations tried to capitalize on this concentration of vessel ownership—emphasizing limited entry into the industry and catch quota systems. The United States, which always had a much more decentralized industrial structure, focused on limiting the type of gear used and closing certain areas to fishing altogether.

These partial regulatory schemes failed partially because they were instituted too late. Worldwatch Institute researcher Anne Platt McGinn has shown that the

RELATIVE DISTRIBUTION AND ABUNDANCE OF COD

Circles indicate cod were present; larger circles indicate more cod.
Plus signs indicate sampled areas where no cod were found.

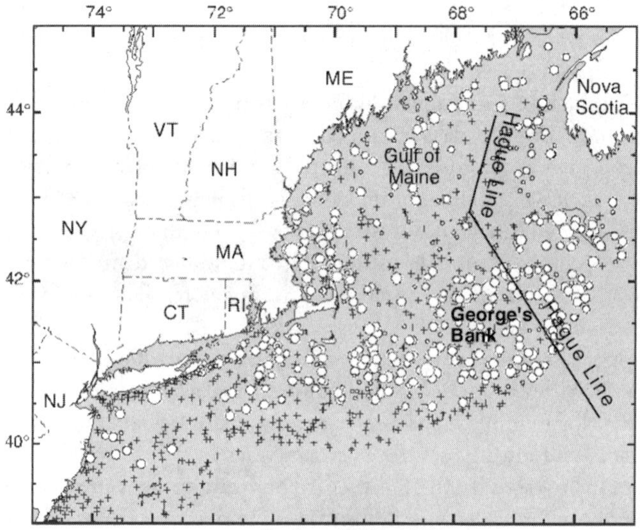

Spring 1979–1981

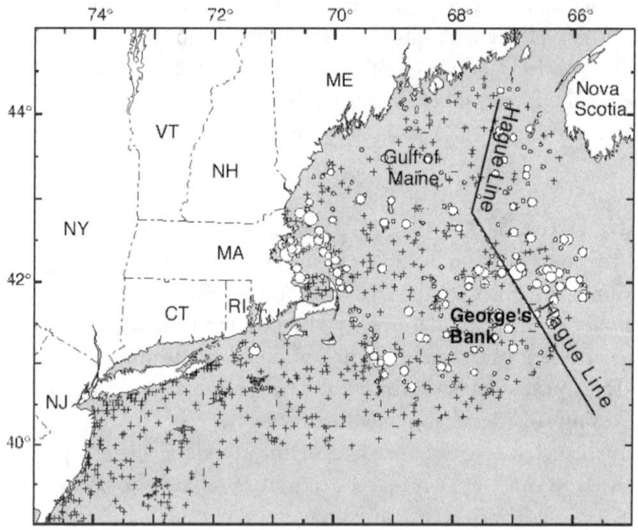

Spring 1997–1999

Maps Credit: Michael Lepera
Source: Northeast Fisheries Science Center <www.nefsc.nmfs.gov>

governments only acted in the face of immediate environmental collapse. To succeed, McGinn argues, regulators would have had to take a precautionary approach—monitoring environmental indicators more closely, and implementing regulations when the indicators pointed to a coming crisis, rather than after the crisis itself had occurred. In the aftermath of failed attempts at regulation, both the United States and Canada resorted to widespread closures of fishing grounds.

The 200-mile limits themselves posed a tremendous obstacle to effective management. The fishing grounds are part of a single ecosystem. To work, any system of regulation would have to address the ecosystem in its entirety. Instead, the 200-mile limits divided the grounds between Canadian and U.S. sovereignty, often in an atmosphere of national fervor and acrimony. This thwarted the development of an overarching authority that could work across boundaries in governing the whole ecosystem.

Perhaps the most uncontrollable of the challenges to effective fisheries management, however, is the voracious world market for fish. Many of the largest seafood producers shop regularly on the international market. Gorton's Foods, for example, is actually located in Gloucester, Massachusetts, but has not used locally landed fish in its products for nearly 30 years. The company relies instead on a world supply of quick-frozen fish that is more readily available and cheaper than the local supply. The world fish market protects the big seafood concerns from fluctuations in the local catch—isolating the impact to the local level. Reductions in a regional catch, whether for ecological or regulatory reasons, do not necessarily mean increased prices for regional fishers, as there are ready substitutes from fisheries around the world. As

U.S. FISH CATCH (THOUSANDS OF METRIC TONS)

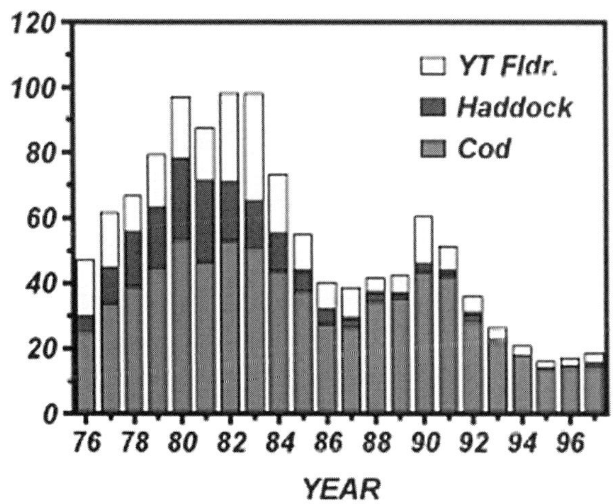

Source: Northeast Fisheries Science Center www.nefsc.nmfs.gov

the traditional Atlantic cod and halibut have disappeared from the fish counters they have been seamlessly replaced with Chilean sea bass, mahi mahi, and other white fish with similar texture and appearance.

Regulations limiting the catch have clashed with the tightly knit culture of professional fishers, sparking resentment among the fishing communities and provoking an unwillingness to comply with the measures imposed. Fishers have continued under their customary mode of operation—pushing their own limits and those of the ecosystem. Today's fishing technology, however, is simply too efficient for the traditional aggressive mode of harvest to be practiced in a sustainable way. If the fisheries are to be restored, the very culture of fishing is going to have to change.

New Approaches

Various proposed regulatory structures have tried to grapple with the fisheries crisis. Maritime anthropologist Evelyn Pinkerton has advocated the novel approach of involving the fishing communities themselves in fisheries management. Numerous case studies show that organizations of fishers can become active participants in the development and enforcement of fisheries policy, with the sustainability of the harvest as a key objective. Salmon fishers in southeastern Alaska, for example, formed an organization that included all types of harvest technologies and worked effectively with state environmental bodies to guarantee the benefits of the industry for all participants—including commercial and sport fishers. Such examples of cooperative fisheries management, while usually working on a small scale, are particularly encouraging because they show fishing communities changing their relationship to their fisheries—from simple harvester to active custodian.

The goal of management of the northwest Atlantic fisheries cannot be to restore fish stocks to a level where intensive fishing can be resumed. This would only perpetuate the fishing culture that has proved so destructive and lead to future environmental disasters and industrial collapse. Introducing restraint into the fishing culture of the northwest Atlantic will probably be the greatest challenge for future regulatory policy. If there is any silver lining to the current crisis, however, it is that the fishers' shared sense of economic desperation could help engender the collective identity necessary for them to assume a central role in the management of the fisheries.

Fisheries management is a global problem with intense local consequences. The depletion of the northwest Atlantic fishing grounds has meant not only economic disaster for local fishing communities, but also increased pressure on other grounds around the world to make up the difference. Managing the fisheries of the northwest Atlantic will require the establishment of an international oversight institution. To sustain the fishing communities that line the shores, the fishers will need to be active and central players in the development and implementation of fisheries policy. If a successful system can be developed, every effort should be made to apply it to other threatened fishing grounds throughout the world's oceans. Ultimately, the role of the fisher will have to be reshaped—from hunter to shepherd of the seas.

Resources: Mark Kurlansky, *Cod: A Biography of the Fish that Changed the World*, 1997; Peter B. Doeringer and David G. Terkla, *Troubled Waters: Economic Structure, Regulatory reform, and Fisheries Trade*, 1995; Anne Platt McGinn, *Rocking the Boat: Conserving Fisheries and Protecting Jobs, Worldwatch Paper 142*, Worldwatch Institute, 1998; Evelyn Pinkerton, ed., *Co-operative Management of Local Fisheries*, 1989; Linda Greenlaw, *The Hungry Ocean: A Swordboat Captain's Journey*, 1999; Sebastian Junger, *The Perfect Storm*, 1997; "Five dead: 'What's happening here?'" *Portland Press Herald*, October 27, 2000.

EXTINCTION IS FOREVER

DEBATING DAMS AND DOLLARS IN THE NORTHWEST SALMON CRISIS

JAN CLAUSEN

May/June 2000

An unlikely combination of business executives, grassroots environmentalists, Pacific Northwest tribal leaders, and state and federal bureaucrats came together last September to sign the death warrant on a dam. The setting was impeccably corporate: the Hilton Hotel in downtown Portland, Oregon. Attire ranged from suits and ties to a whimsical t-shirt depicting hands raised in tribute to a soaring salmon with the caption "Fish Worship: Is It Wrong?" A man from a group called Wild Salmon Nation arrived lugging a huge model fish with detachable scales.

Yakama Nation tribal chair William Yallup opened the proceedings with a traditional prayer. Next up were industry flacks and government bureaucrats mouthing upbeat clichés. In closing, the assembly joined in singing a version of the Neil Young tune "Long May You Run," with lyrics extolling free-flowing rivers.

The ceremony marked the signing of an agreement to remove Condit Dam, a small hydroelectric facility near the mouth of Washington State's White Salmon River, a tributary of the Columbia. Since its construction in 1913, Condit has blocked salmon and steelhead trout from reaching historic spawning grounds. Fish advocates view the agreement as one small step toward resolving a massive environmental crisis that has wiped out Pacific Northwest salmon in almost 40% of the rivers where they spawn and put the salmon at risk of extinction in close to half of the remaining streams.

The salmon's problems stem from a complex series of environmental changes brought by a rapidly developing industrial economy. Overfishing, increasing demand on water supplies, and the impact of careless logging and agricultural practices all play a role. But one of the biggest fish killers in the Columbia River Basin is the gauntlet of hydroelectric dams that anadromous fish including salmon must run. Anadromous fish are born and die in fresh water but spend much of their lives in the ocean. In order to reproduce, they must survive the dams twice—once when they are juveniles, or smolts, making their journey to the ocean, and again when they return to spawn and die precisely where their lives began.

Although Condit is small potatoes as Northwest dams go, it is the tallest of the nation's dams currently slated for demolition, and the symbolism of the removal agreement is significant in a region furiously embroiled in the politics of fish rescue. Much of the politicking centers on practical economic concerns, but under the guise of disagreements over bottom-line issues the protagonists also are skirmishing over competing models of economic well-being. Fundamentally, they are debating the appropriate relationship between people and nature, and revealing the limits of a conceptual system that ignores forms of wealth not reducible to dollars.

Confronting the Killing Fields

Ground zero in the debate over the costs and benefits of saving salmon is a proposal to remove four federally owned and operated hydroelectric dams on the lower Snake River in eastern Washington. The Snake River, the mighty Columbia's largest tributary, was once the breeding ground for about half of the anadromous fish in the four-state Columbia Basin. After the Ice Harbor, Lower Monumental, Little Goose, and Lower Granite dams were built in the 1960s and '70s, fish populations declined alarmingly. Over the past three decades, the Snake has lost nearly 90% of its wild anadromous fish. Snake River coho salmon were declared extinct in 1986. In 1991, Snake River sockeye became the first variety of Pacific salmon to be listed under the Endangered Species Act.

The four dams on the lower river have created what Alaska Governor Tony Knowles recently dubbed "killing fields." Expensive efforts to mitigate the impact have failed utterly. And most scientists concur that taking out the dams would offer the best chance for fish recovery.

Yet their sheer size and economic importance far exceeds that of other dams considered for demolition, making their removal a far from simple matter. Together, the four facilities generate about 5% of the Northwest's electricity and create a sluggish channel allowing shipping on a 140-mile stretch of the Snake River between Pasco, Washington, and Lewiston, Idaho.

Driving much of the official urgency to save the fish is the Endangered Species Act. Treaties giving local tribes the right to harvest fish also play an important role. In addition, a broad segment of the general public shares the alarm expressed in the environmentalist's slogan: Extinction is forever. Love for salmon isn't confined to tree-hugging types; people who regard "environmentalists" as a slur often revel in sports fishing and savor barbecued salmon, giving anadromous fish a cachet that has eluded less-beloved yet no-less-endangered species like the spotted owl.

The Native American community became an early advocate of lower Snake dam removal. In 1995, The Columbia River Inter-Tribal Fish Commission, which represents four tribes with fishing rights in the Columbia system, proposed returning the

Snake River to its natural flow. As the idea gathered support, it brought expressions of dismay from the region's politicians. Nevertheless, the dams operator, the U.S. Army Corps of Engineers, has spent the last three years studying whether to retire the four dams by breaching their earthen portions, allowing the river to flow around the remaining concrete structures. ("Breaching" involves partial removal of the dam to allow fish passage, without removing the concrete.) The Corps has been joined by a bewildering array of government agencies presided over by the National Marine Fisheries Service, whose mission it is to interpret Endangered Species Act provisions. Should the agencies recommend that the dams be decommissioned, Congress would still have to approve the plan.

The debate over removing the Snake River dams will test not only the region's, but the nation's willingness to discard the old notion that any free-flowing river is a "wasted" resource. That notion has deep roots in frontier history, which can be described as a lengthy series of schemes for extracting wealth from nature. In the Northwest, it received a big boost from the New Deal initiative to create massive federal dam projects for popular purposes. Explaining the passion with which many defend the dams, policy analyst Steve Weiss of the Northwest Energy Coalition, a Seattle based environmental group, points to an impending paradigm shift: "It's a culture clash over, 'Do we dominate the environment or do we live in it? Can we do techno fixes, or must nature do it?'"

The Challenge From Native Americans

No group has challenged the mainstream paradigm more radically than Pacific Northwest tribes for whom salmon figures as both a crucial economic resource and a central element of spiritual and ceremonial life. Tribal fish advocates are calling into question both the measurement of wealth exclusively in dollars and the assumption that economic benefit requires the technological manipulation of nature.

The short shrift given the tribes' interests provides a vivid example of social bias masquerading as pragmatic economic calculation. As Steve Weiss sees it, dams have widespread backing because they symbolize "white men taming the Wild West," while tribes and nontribal fisherfolk lack sufficient "iconic status" to have their stake in the fate of salmon taken seriously.

"Everyone talks about what farmers will lose or what other groups will lose if we take out the dams, but nobody talks about what Indians will lose if the fish go extinct," says Donald Sampson, executive director of the Columbia River Inter-Tribal Fish Commission. Sampson, who's in his late thirties, is a university-trained fisheries biologist and former chair of the Umatilla Confederated Tribes. He can be refreshingly irreverent, savoring jokes about ingenious ways of eliminating dam-favoring politicians and mocking federal bureaucrats for their "paralysis by analysis." But there's no mistaking his gravity when he describes tribal successes in restoring naturally reproducing salmon runs on the Umatilla River or explains how traditional ceremonies strengthen the bonds between salmon and tribal people. Even tribal members who fish commercially, he says, have respect for the fish, such that "you never hear an Indian talk about 'that critter,' 'that dumb critter,' the way non-Indians do." Historically, he maintains, tribal people recognized their responsibility to manage their relationship to the land not just for the group's immediate benefit but for coming generations.

Clearly, Sampson is talking about a concept of material well-being that is at odds with the prevailing bottom-line mentality. But even when making bottom-line calculations, much could be done to correct built-in biases in the very terms that typically structure economic analyses of "improvements" to the natural order. A recent article in the journal Environmental Law making the legal case for dam breaching draws attention to this problem: "Frequently … the perceived benefits of dams are fully quantified and overstated, while the costs are greatly understated and ignored. Traditional cost-benefit analysis did not calculate true social costs, such as environmental damage … and support subsidies."

Putting a Dollar Value on Salmon

In an attempt to fill in some of these gaps, the U.S. Army Corps of Engineers estimated the "existence value" of salmon in an evaluation of various conservation measures. This move has been controversial.

Many people doubt the reliability of answers given to the question, "What would you pay to know that salmon exist?" Enviros often feel uneasy about the pressure to express even the value of nature as a monetary calculation, yet the salmon's urgent plight draws them into the game of putting a price tag on 10 million years of evolution (the amount of time the close anadromous relatives of today's Pacific salmon have been around).

Taking a different approach, the Columbia River treaty tribes have refused to calculate the dollar value of the species whose survival they see as integrally connected to their own identity and the well being of the Earth.

In effect, they are refusing to separate spiritual values from material interests, thereby challenging the cherished European-American concept of "the economy" as a law unto itself. I asked Charles Hudson, the tribal fish commission's public information manager, to explain this stand. "In our minds," he responded, "you only begin the argument with tens of billions of dollars. If it came to extinction, how would you ever put a dollar amount on the institutional racism involved? Treaty rights are not a negotiable item."

Yet Hudson also stresses that, for tribal members on reservations where jobs are scarce, fishing often constitutes the only "homegrown and traditional" source of income. He speaks angrily of the unjust "wealth transfer" in both the 19th and 20th centuries: the resource that created the tribes' pretreaty prosperity was decimated so that rivers could generate income for settlers. The tribes possessed real wealth even though they didn't subscribe to Western concepts of private property.

Hudson's analysis of wealth transfer reveals how the poverty now so widespread among indigenous people stems from economic choices made by settlers and their heirs. By reminding us that there recently existed on North American soil a functioning model of the good life that had nothing to do with capitalist relations of production (or even a cash economy), the tribes powerfully contradict the deadly force of TINA, the disabling suspicion that There Is No Alternative to existing economic arrangements. They nudge us to look beyond the restrictive framework that equates all "real" material values with marketplace transactions.

Dollar Costs and Benefits

While the tribes push the mainstream cultural envelope by insisting on their treaty rights, nontribal enviros work hard to show how removing the dams can work in today's economy. The dams' defenders, led by powerful Washington Republican Senator Slade Gorton, have loudly forecast economic disaster ever since the plan was first aired, and thus far no one in the Northwest's congressional delegation has had the courage to come out in favor of breaching. (Oregon's Democratic governor, John Kitzhaber, did take a strong stand in favor of the removal plan this past February).

The politicians' preference for the status quo is unsurprising given that cheap hydroelectric power has long been the backbone of the Northwest's industrial economy. Industrialists with no direct stake in the four lower Snake dams apparently subscribe to a sort of economic domino theory, fearing that even a localized move to prioritize salmon might encourage public scrutiny of the high environmental costs of present patterns of river usage. Such fears surfaced during negotiations over the Condit Dam removal agreement, with Condit's private owner, PacifiCorp, insisting that the agreement not be construed as setting any precedents.

Economic Enfranchisement Through Dams

By no means do all the dams' champions hail from the corridors of power. East of the Cascade Mountains—the range the divides the Northwest's rainy coastal region from the dry interior—many families of modest means have long relied on federal subsidies rooted in FDR's Depression era vision of vast public works that would create opportunities for the dispossessed. That dependence can turn support for dams into a quasi-theological principle. Blaine Harden, an eastern Washington native who calls himself "a legatee of the conquered river," writes of the dam-related "federal dollars that rained for decades [giving] me and my family work, water, electricity, and pride in ourselves."

For some, dams are literally a theological matter, to judge from a diatribe posted on the website *saveourdams.com*. The author denounces "the 'New Age Religion'" whose followers "believe in earth first and want to return the earth to the way it was before man set foot upon it. They believe in the created above the creator and they want to do this at any cost."

Like Governor Kitzhaber, he and other activists stress the importance of planning for effective ways to cushion localized negative effects. In fact, monetary costs and benefits of breaching are roughly in balance, according to a recent analysis by the Northwest Energy Coalition drawing on government-sponsored studies. The real problem is that the change would disadvantage certain groups while benefiting others. As Governor Kitzhaber of Oregon points out, the challenge thus becomes "to develop an ecosystem recovery strategy that spreads the costs as broadly as possible," including the costs of mitigating negative economic impacts.

Despite the difficult political climate, Bill Arthur, Northwest Regional Director of the Sierra Club, believes that the dam-removal debate is beginning to follow the trajectory of the region's ancient forest controversy, with doomsday predictions gradually giving way to a narrower focus on real problems and manageable solutions. Like Governor Kitzhaber, he and other activists stress the importance of planning for effective ways to cushion negative economic impacts. According to Tim Stearns of Save Our Wild Salmon, "We [environmentalists] have done most of the economic transition stuff that the administration should have done."

For example, American Rivers commissioned a retired Army Corps of Engineers official to examine ways to restructure the region's transportation system in anticipation of the day when farmers will no longer be able to ship their crops by barge on the Snake River between Lewiston, Idaho and Pasco, Washington. He found uncompetitive pricing among shippers and hidden taxpayer subsidies of about $30 million a year to operate the lower Snake waterway. Given appropriate investment in transportation infrastructure, enviros argue, shipping farm goods by road or rail instead of by water could actually strengthen the agricultural economy. Senator Gorton blasted the study as "more voodoo economics from another D.C.-based special interest group."

Those most likely to benefit from dam removal in bottom-line terms include tribes, rail and trucking firms, the nontribal commercial fishing industry, private power companies, and the recreation industry. One knowledgeable enviro told me that official projections of the dollar benefits of dam removal to the recreation industry got revised drastically downward before the findings were released. The original estimate, which seems to have scared the feds, indicated a net yearly increase of $1 billion in recreation-related activity with a free-flowing river.

In addition to higher transportation costs, the potential economic downside of breaching includes loss of jobs related to operating the dams and the river ports they create; diminished irrigation opportunities; higher electrical rates throughout the Northwest; and the actual costs of the bypassing operation, which have been estimated between $800 million and $1.1 billion. Economists propose a buyout of the 13 corporate farms that rely on Ice Harbor Dam for irrigation water.

The cost of the breaching would amount to about $25 million per year above the current operating budget of the Bonneville Power Administration (BPA), which sells electricity from a complex of federally owned dams including those on the lower Snake. Its customers would probably absorb most of this cost. (By comparison, the BPA's customers still pay $500 million annually on the enormous debt left over from a disastrous nuclear-power venture that collapsed in the 1980s.)

Dismantling the four lower Snake dams would cause electrical rates to rise moderately, though the Northwest would continue to enjoy the cheapest power in the nation. The BPA's worst case estimate shows a 10% increase for ratepayers whose bills are currently 40% below the national average.

While the lost electricity could readily be replaced on the open energy market, where power often comes from "dirty" coal- and oil-fired plants or somewhat cleaner gas, enviros are pushing for a combination of conservation (to reduce energy demand) and power from renewable sources such as wind, solar, or geothermal power. Opponents of dam removal appear to hope that the need for unpleasant change will simply go away if they scuttle the breaching plan. But the cautious Oregonian, whose editorial page routinely insists that the dams can coexist with the salmon recovery, recently concluded that no credible effort to improve fish survival will be any cheaper than partial removal. For instance, Idaho would face a severe drop in irrigation water if stream flows increased to aid fish. The lost irrigation could eliminate as many as 6,500 jobs and $430 million in income, according to Rob Masonis of American Rivers. The region as a whole would have to cope with unpopular restrictions on logging, farming, and development. And nontribal economists have calculated that extinction of the Snake River's anadromous stocks—more likely if dams remain—could cost U.S. taxpayers $12 billion or more in compensation to tribes with treaty fishing rights. Given such considerations, Governor Kitzhaber argues that breaching will distribute the economic burden of saving salmon more equitably than other credible fish-recovery plans.

National Implications

Recently, environmental groups and tribes have taken the debate over the salmon crisis to the national level, running ads in *The New York Times* aimed at prodding Al Gore to justify his "green" reputation by making dam removal an issue in his presidential campaign. The word is out to members of eastern and midwestern Congressional delegations that the Northwest's cherished energy price advantage must not continue at the cost of decimating endangered species and that the best available scientific studies forecast extinction of Snake River salmon by 2017 absent effective intervention.

With Gore unresponsive and the National Marine Fisheries Service evidently prepared literally to study the fish to death rather than make politically difficult decisions, Tim Stearns of Save Our Wild Salmon inquires with more than a touch of exasperation, "If they don't like dam removal, what do they like?"

His question reverberates with national implications. In reporting on the agreement to remove Condit Dam, the local and national press noted a widespread questioning of the historic assumption that "harnessing" rivers for energy and irrigation is always beneficial. The press connected the Condit story to the case of Edwards Dam, a 24-foot-high hydropower facility on Maine's Kennebec River. This dam was recently demolished at the behest of the Federal Energy Regulatory Commission to restore native fish.

Big dams still look like progress to a lot of people but every day more of us are recognizing that healthy environments need free-flowing water. In the process, we are rethinking the appropriate role of human beings in modifying natural systems. Assessing the stakes in the Snake River debate, Northwest Energy Coalition policy analyst Steve Weiss sums up, "It's one battle [over] a huge paradigm of 'how do we live on this planet?' Whatever happens will change the playing field."

CHAPTER 5

ENVIRONMENTAL PROTECTION AND THE DEVELOPING WORLD

FOOL'S GOLD

TEN PROBLEMS WITH GOLD MINING

PROJECT UNDERGROUND

July/August 2001

Over 85% of gold mined today will end up as jewelry tomorrow. Gold mining is not an essential industry like the harvesting of food or even paper production. It is certainly not sustainable, nor is it just. Yet the cumulative impacts of gold mining worldwide, on local economies and ecosystems, are at least as bad as those of industrial forestry and agribusiness. With more than 66% of all new mining exploration in the hard-rock sector currently focused on gold, the problems are going to get worse for people and places around the planet. Here's why:

One: Genocide

Every major gold rush has meant death and devastation for local people at the hands of fortune-seekers. California's Native American nations were decimated first by the diseases the 49ers brought with them, then by the new California state government, which put bounties on the heads of native people. Today the Galamsey of West Africa, the Igorot of the Philippines, and the Macuxi and Yanomami of the Amazon are similarly endangered. The Yanomami, for example, had little contact with the rest of

Brazil until the arrival of the first garimpeiros (gold miners) in the 1970s. By 1989, an estimated 40,000 miners had flocked to the area, polluting rivers and spreading malaria. Decimated by disease, the number of Yanomamis living in Brazil (many also live in Venezuela) fell from 20,000 to about 8,000 in just 20 years. In the words of Yanomami representative Davi Kopenawa Yanomami, "What we do not want are the mining companies, which destroy the forest, and the garimpeiros, who bring so many diseases. These whites must respect our Yanomami land. The garimpeiros bring guns, alcohol, prostitution, and destroy nature wherever they go. The machines spill oil into the rivers and kill the life existing in them and the people and animals who depend on them. For us, this is not progress."

Two: Water

Damage to water and water resources is the worst environmental consequence of gold mining. From California's Sierra Nevada in the 1850s to the lands of the Pemon in Venezuela today, people have ruined rivers by using high-pressure hoses to spray down the banks and sifting through the sediment for gold. Runoff flows downstream, destroying plant and fish life. But modern mining is even more destructive of water resources: the gold industry in Nevada—where most gold in the United States is mined—consumes more water than all the people in the state. The water table has fallen as much as 1,000 feet around some of the largest open-pit gold mines in northeastern Nevada, according to the U.S. Geological Survey. One of the mines consumes 100 million gallons per day—as much as the city of Austin, Texas. And that's not all: Water systems around mines are contaminated by cyanide and other processing chemicals, and the acid mine drainage that runs off exposed rock.

Three: Waste Rock

To make a simple gold wedding band, at least 2.8 tons of earth are excavated. The gold-mining industry generates an enormous amount of waste compared to its product: The 2,402 tons of gold produced in 1997 resulted in 725 million tons of waste, which was contaminated with metals, acids, and solvents, according to Worldwatch Institute. The standard ratio of waste production in the U.S. gold-mining industry is one to three million, meaning that for every ton of gold produced there are three million tons of waste rock. Most of the unsightly mess left behind is exposed to weathering and will ultimately leach acid and heavy metals into the local area at great ecological cost.

Four: Corporate Welfare

In many countries, gold-mining companies are allowed "free entry" to public lands for mineral exploitation. In the United States, it is not entirely free—but the companies only pay $5 an acre to "patent" a patch of federal land and open it to mining. Since 1872, the government has "sold" land equivalent in size to the state of Connecticut under this law. This land contained $245 billion worth of minerals! Pushed by corporate advisors, developing countries are adopting similar land policies as well. Since 1994, more than 70 countries have changed their laws to attract foreign gold-mining companies. As a result, the gold-mining industry in the global South is booming: Between 1991 and 1997, exploration investments doubled in Africa, quadrupled in the Pacific region, and expanded by six times in Latin America. Since a "pro-development" mining act was adopted in 1995 in the Philippines, over a quarter of the country's land surface has been handed over as gold mining prospects.

Five: Indigenous Rights

In the United States—the world's second biggest gold producer—more than 70% of gold is ripped from native lands. The Western Shoshone, whose traditional domain covers most of Nevada, are the unhappy hosts to more than three dozen open-pit gold mines on their land, many at least a mile wide and a mile deep, with toxic ponds at the bottom. The U.S. government has continually denied the Western Shoshone their land and treaty rights, as it increasingly allocates Nevada's lands to multinational mining. The story repeats itself around the globe. In Ghana, in the mid-1990s, thousands of traditional farmers were evicted and replaced by World Bank-sponsored gold mining operations covering hundreds of square kilometers. It is now estimated that 50% of gold produced in the next 20 years will come from indigenous peoples' lands.

Six: Cyanide

Cyanide is the chemical of choice for mining companies to extract gold from crushed ore. Very low-grade ore, with minimal residues of gold, is crushed and piled on the ground, then sprayed with a cyanide solution. No mine has ever avoided leaking cyanide into the ecosystem. In 1998, a cyanide spill on a Canadian-owned gold mine in Kyrgyzstan resulted in four deaths and the evacuation of thousands of people living downstream. At one southern Colorado mine, Summitville, taxpayers have already paid out $100 million for the Environmental Protection Agency (EPA) to simply contain—not clean up—contamination of local rivers.

Seven: Mercury

For centuries, mercury has been used to chemically separate gold from ore, leading to major public-health problems for miners and communities around mining districts. During the California Gold Rush, 7,600 tons of mercury were released into local rivers and lakes, resulting in neurological disorders and deaths amongst people exposed to this deadly toxin. More than 50% of mercury exposure today in the San Francisco

Bay area is an historic legacy of the 1849 gold rush. Furthermore, millions of small-scale miners use mercury, from the Amazon—where they have invaded indigenous reservations—to the Philippines, resulting in the worst recent outbreaks of Minamata (or "Mad Hatter's") disease. Of 500,000 gold miners tested in Brazil, more than 30% showed mercury levels above the World Health Organization's tolerable limits.

Eight: Dowry

Nearly 80% of gold is sold as jewelry, most of it in India. In 1998, the country's gold consumption added up to 815 metric tons, nearly twice that of the United States. This is not, however, a simple tale of vanity or excessive consumption. It is part of the dowry women pay for a man's hand in marriage. Activists working around the gold industry aim both to redress the abuses of mining for communities living in mineral producing areas, and to challenge the patriarchy that forces women to hold gold as their only fallback in times of scarcity. Indian women and activists fighting the dowry system are becoming increasingly aware of the dangers of gold production worldwide. As long as there is pressure on Indian women to own gold, however, it can be derived from non-virgin production. Gold in the vaults of the "developed world" could feed the demand even for India's market for years to come.

Nine: Dud Investment

According to Merrill Lynch, gold is "the duddest of dud investments." Ever since the U.S. dollar went off the gold standard, gold has had no special value as a commodity, with only 280 tons going to industrial uses per year. Yet some people continue to hoard it. The price of gold has been slowly dropping and is now well below the price of its production at many modern mines, which means companies mining new or "virgin" gold are a bad investment. Even the 35,000 tons of gold bullion held in central banks have lost 30% of their value over the last decade—a huge waste of taxpayer assets. Some governments are already beginning to sell off their gold reserves. In the last five years, the Argentine, Australian, Belgian, British, Canadian, Dutch, and Swiss central banks have sold large quantities of gold, as has the International Monetary Fund, causing the price of gold to plummet.

Ten: Ecosystem Impacts

Contamination and waste of water, destruction of habitat and biodiversity, industrialization of wilderness, road-building, and waste-dumping in mined areas all negatively impact the environment around gold mines. "Frontier forests"—the last remaining old growth stands—are under siege from gold exploration. Fisheries suffer from heavy siltation and toxic run-off into waterways from gold mines. Today, mines scrape away and dig up more earth than do the world's rivers through natural erosion! The impact on wildlife is hard to calculate, but between 1980 and 1990 seven thousand birds were found dead near cyanide-laced ponds at gold mines in California, Nevada, and Arizona—the tip of the iceberg of gold mine-related wildlife deaths.

SUSTAINABLE SANITATION
A GLOBAL HEALTH CHALLENGE
LAURA ORLANDO
May/June 2001

In late October 1995, in the small town of Greenland, New Hampshire, Wheelabrator Water Technologies, Inc. dumped 650 tons of sewage sludge on Rosamond Hughes' field. The sludge contained not only the dregs left over from sewage treatment but also 700 pounds of a nitrogen-based polymer (used to remove water from sludge) and 24,000 pounds of lime. After sitting for several days, the sludge was chain-dragged across the field's surface with a tractor, and then spread repeatedly for the next three weeks. As it dried, it was blown by steady winds toward the home of 26-year-old Shayne Conner, just 300 feet away.

Almost immediately, Conner, his family, and their neighbors began to get sick. Overcome by the stench, they started vomiting. They felt burning sensations in their eyes, throats, and lungs. They experienced nosebleeds, headaches, congestion, fever, and nausea, and they had difficulty breathing. And then, on a quiet day in November—less than one month after the sludge was dumped on the Hughes' property—Shayne Conner died.

When sanitation is practiced successfully, it can promote health and prevent disease. But its effectiveness depends on many factors—education, behavioral changes, access to clean water, solid and industrial waste management, and the safe disposition of human excreta. What happened to Shayne Conner is just one tragic example of how, in rich as well as poor countries, improper sanitation can cause environmental degradation, illness, and death.

Rich Nation, Poor Sanitation

In rich countries, sewers and sewage treatment systems are considered signs of progress, but they are the reason we have toxic sludge. First comes the sewage, a mixture of undifferentiated industrial and household wastes. Then there's the treatment process, which attempts to clean the wastewater that the sewage contains. What's left over—after the dead cats and cardboard are screened out and hauled away to the dump—is a concoction of whatever was flushed down the drain: motor oil, dioxin, asbestos, polychlorinated biphenyls (PCBs), heavy metals, bacteria, viruses, industrial solvents, any combination of the 70,000 chemicals used in U.S. industries, and so on. And the better the water at the end of the treatment cycle, the nastier the sludge will be.

At one time, sludge's pungent smell was considered offensive only on aesthetic grounds. But new research in the *Journal of Agromedicine* confirms that sludge's olfactory assault can have serious physical health consequences as well. So, while it might seem safe and convenient to have our waste whisked out of sight, we're paying the piper at the end of the pipe.

In spite of sludge's poisonous properties, the federal government keeps calling it a fertilizer and putting it on land. The Environmental Protection Agency (EPA) is in charge of regulating the disposal of sewage sludge. Since 1992, when Congress banned the practice of dumping sludge in the ocean, the EPA has geared its regulations and public relations efforts toward one goal: To dump sludge wherever possible, primarily on U.S. farmland. That's the cheapest way to dispose of sludge and launder the toxic waste that goes into sewers. The EPA now goes to great lengths to convince people that sludge makes good fertilizer. For instance, the agency refers to sludge as "biosolids"—the winning entry in a 1990 contest sponsored by the sewage industry to make its main product more marketable.

Despite the preponderance of pro-sludge propaganda, however, not everyone is fooled. When Shayne Conner's mother, Joanne Marshall, filed a wrongful death suit against Wheelabrator, Dr. David Lewis—an EPA microbiologist and whistleblower—testified in the case. According to Lewis, the symptoms reported by Greenland, New Hampshire, residents were "consistent with a growing number of cases where people have been exposed to airborne contaminants from land-applied sewage sludge." It was well-established in the scientific and medical literature, Lewis noted, that "inhaling of irritant gases and pathogen-contaminated, limed sludge dust" could "lead to infections of respiratory and gastrointestinal systems and serious, life-threatening complications."

Why, then, is the United States so invested in the sewers and sewage treatment plants that produce toxic sludge? Since passage of the Clean Water Act in 1972, many communities have had no choice but to put in sewers and build expensive sewage treatment plants. The resulting multi-billion dollar sewering effort created a powerful wastewater industry. The EPA, while ostensibly charged with protecting the environment, caters to that industry and other corporate interests.

What we do with sludge now is a public health and environmental disaster. Instead, sludge should be treated as hazardous waste. We need to promote public policies that aim to reduce its production, by not extending existing sewers or building new ones. In addition, source separation should be the mantra of the EPA (and you and me): Keeping waste products separate at the point of production will greatly facilitate safe recycling and reuse.

Sanitation Crisis in the Global South

In the wealthiest country in the world, people are dying from the industrial end product of state-of-the-art sewage treatment systems. In the Global South, where 65% of the population have no sanitation facilities at all, people are dying from exposure to excreta that carry disease.

The state of global sanitation, according to Akhtar Hameed Khan, is "unconscionable." Khan is the director of the Orangi Pilot Project, a low-cost sanitation project that has reached thousands of people in Karachi, Pakistan. "On the brink of the 21st century," he wrote in *Progress of Nations*, a 1997 UNICEF study, "half the world's people are enduring a medieval level of sanitation. Almost 3 billion individuals do not have access to a decent toilet, and many of them are forced to defecate on the bare ground or queue up to pay for the use of a filthy latrine."

The "medieval level of sanitation," Khan points out, results in a "medieval level of disease." The improper management of human excreta wreaks havoc on people's health in both rich and poor countries. But its consequences are most brutal for poor people in developing nations, where it results in the deaths of 2.2 million children each year. In densely settled areas where there is no containment of human waste, disease-causing organisms—primarily found in feces—easily move from one person to the next. (Water is the ideal but by no means the only conduit.) These organisms cause many illnesses, including diarrhoeal diseases, which are responsible for killing the majority of children who die before reaching the age of five. In addition to promulgating disease and degrading water and soil quality, the lack of ecological excreta management is a dignity issue in people's everyday lives.

When it comes to investing in environment sanitation, however, bringing health and dignity to poor people is not high on the list. The lion's share of such investment goes to sewerage in urban areas, subsidizing services for industrial development, the middle class, and the rich. According to the United Nations, in 2000, only 34% of rural residents in developing countries had access to sanitation, compared with 80% of urban residents. During the UN-declared International Water and Sanitation Decade (1980-1990), funding for sanitation skyrocketed. But according to Frank Hartvelt, deputy director of the Science and Technology Private Sector Division of the UN Development Programme, 80% of all investment went to "well-off urban areas, for expensive installations." As in wealthy countries, it is those with the most economic clout who decide what kinds of public services will be provided, and who will benefit from the expenditure of public funds.

These same priorities determine what types of solutions the world's sanitation "experts" devise. In 1998, the UN set up the World Water Commission to examine water issues. In its *Vision Report,* published last year, the Commission identified what it called "a vital need for high tech innovation." As an example of this, the *Report* suggested "the use of computer chips to control the digestion process in smart-composting toilets." Good for Intel—bad for the three billion people without any toilet. The digestion process in composting toilets needs carbon—chopped leaves, wood chips—not silicon. But then again, they wouldn't be able to add and subtract.

People in the Global South live in a world rich enough to afford a universal level of sanitation that would help to protect their health. But regardless of how much money is available, we will trade one set of problems for another unless we radically rethink how that money is spent.

A Model for Sustainable Sanitation

The truth is, neither sewers nor computer chips in composting toilets are functionally or environmentally sustainable. Instead, what is needed are sanitation systems that keep toxic and human wastes separate, prevent pollution, and return the nutrients in urine and feces to the soil as fertilizers. (See sidebar.) Small projects have demonstrated systems that accomplish these goals while also being culturally appropriate, locally responsible, affordable, functional, and even beautiful.

One example can be found on the Caribbean coast of Mexico, a fragile ecosystem that is home to 554,000 people and four million tourists. Since 1993, the ReSource Institute for Low Entropy Systems (RILES), a nonprofit concerned with sanitation, has built about 300 composting toilets in the Yucatan Peninsula. Most are paid for by their owners: maids, gardeners, masons, carpenters, schoolteachers, doctors, editors, tourism operators, hotels, municipalities, and retired Americans, to name a few. All of them are functioning well. Word has spread that they have no smell, do not fill up, can be in the house or outside, and can be hooked to a water toilet or not; that there is somebody around who knows how to maintain them; and that there are people who will gladly take away and use the fertilizer that these systems produce. The fact that these composting toilets are also beautiful is no small part of their success. The first few were built in houses with dirt floors, but soon people with beachfront homes wanted them. Because of their aesthetic appeal, the toilets have won acceptance across class boundaries. In an effort to build a local infrastructure to keep up with demand and maintain quality control, RILES has helped establish three Mexican corporations: a company to prefabricate the composting toilets; a workers' cooperative to maintain them and build the bathrooms that go on top; and a nonprofit organization to carry out education and policy-related work. (The author is director of RILES.)

Another project is in Cuernavaca, in central Mexico, where an architect named César Añorvé has been promoting two chamber (double-vault) dry toilets. (One chamber is used until full, then left to dehydrate while the other is used.) Añorvé has added an entrepreneurial element to his efforts by designing and selling attractive toilet fixtures. He collaborates with a nonprofit organization, Espacio de Salud, and together they have made the double-vault toilet widely available, with the construction supervision and maintenance necessary to build them correctly and keep them functioning properly.

Why not just hand out blueprints and leave it at that? It doesn't work. It has been demonstrated over and over again that there is an infinite number of ways to build a composting toilet so that it does not function well. Training and supervision take care of this. Regular maintenance keeps the toilets working. Homeowners need support for these things. Add to this the fact that there is a social change element to

HOW DOES A COMPOSTING TOILET WORK?

Human excreta—urine and feces—can be treated one of two ways, either aerobically (with oxygen) or anaerobically (without oxygen). The objectives of treatment are to contain this material, eliminate disease-causing organisms (pathogens), and—in ecological systems like composting toilets—return the nutrients to the soil.

There are different styles of composting toilets—some are built on site and others are commercially manufactured—but all have these objectives in common. For instance, a single chamber composting toilet contains excreta, toilet paper, and even kitchen food waste, in a tank below the bathroom floor. There, biological activity, much like that found in a backyard compost pile, aerobically digests this material. During the treatment process, up to 90% of the volume is driven out of the ventilation stack as carbon dioxide and water. What remains is called *humus*, a fertilizer that looks and smells like the kind of soil you would find in a greenhouse or on a Lancaster farm.

Time, not heat, kills pathogens in the tank. Pathogens generally need their human host to survive. But it's the highly competitive environment in the tank, where they cannot compete with the composting organisms, that does them in. This takes time, which the composting toilet has because of proper sizing and volume reduction. Compost is not removed for years. The urine, on the other hand, is available in days, after passing through a nitrification process inside the treatment tank. It becomes an odorless, stable, nitrogen-rich fertilizer capable, for instance, of doubling corn yields.

The maintenance involved is simple but necessary for proper functioning. It includes maintaining airflow in the tank, periodically adding a bulking agent like coarse sawdust, and removing and using the compost and liquid fertilizer.

the project, and you can see why a blueprint won't do the trick.

Though do-it-yourself construction can be an effective way to get some on-site systems built for low-income households, many other components are needed to bring these efforts to scale. Providing sustainable sanitation technologies for billions of people will require replacing the existing engineering and financial infrastructure that currently supports sewerage with one that supports ecological innovations in waste treatment. That, in turn, will require massive government and organizational—for-profit sometimes, nonprofit other times, a combination of both most of the time—intervention. And whatever the technology, people will have to want it.

What is needed is a new approach consisting of:

- Principles that put source separation first in the decision-making hierarchy;
- People who approach sanitation from both a health and ecological perspective;
- Financing—both private and public—to develop production and marketing capabilities;
- Easy access by those who want sustainable sanitation technologies to those who can deliver, install, and maintain them;
- Financial packages to help people pay for toilets; and
- Government policies that punish polluters, reward ecological innovators, and promote and help pay for universal sustainable sanitation coverage.

The fact that half of the people in the world do not have a toilet reflects government priorities that are politically and morally bankrupt. The fact that the other half has little or no access to sustainable sanitation reflects misconceptions about conventional sanitation systems and what they can and cannot do. Under the current system, everyone suffers. But it doesn't have to be that way.

FINANCING ENVIRONMENTAL MODERATION IN CHINA

DANIEL DELISI

September/October 2000

In 1995, Xi Zhinong, a nature photographer from rural Yunnan Province, started a campaign to save the old-growth forests along the Yunnan-Tibet border. Despite Xi's outspoken criticism of prevailing environmental policies and local logging companies, the campaign gained government support, halting corporate logging in the area. Xi has since founded the Yunnan Conservation Association, a province-wide environmental organization. While environmental problems are certainly not new in China, Xi's campaign created a new activist presence on environmental issues. Like many Chinese environmental activists, Xi faces a tough dilemma—the need to organize for political reform and an inability to fund that activity. He remains, however, an outspoken environmental critic.

In Beijing, where environmentalists have access to international corporate capital, a different story has unfolded. Beginning in 1996, Western corporations, such as Royal Dutch Shell, approached China's oldest and most influential environmental group, Friends of Nature, to organize "joint programs." The effect was immediate. Later that year, Friends of Nature organized its members to attend a lecture on the endangered wild camel in Inner Mongolia. The Wild Camel Foundation, sponsored by Shell, spent an hour gaining the sympathy of the environmentally conscious audience members. When the event finished, attendees received a plastic Shell Oil bag filled with information on the company's vast environmental efforts. A few months later, Friends of Nature organized its members for an Exxon-sponsored Earth Day garbage pick-up on the property surrounding Beijing's elite "Capital Club."

Public Relations and Political Access

The irony is inescapable. Activists all over the world lambaste Shell for polluting Nigeria and supporting the country's military dictatorship. Meanwhile, Friends of Nature founder and president Liang Congjie has Shell China's Public Affairs Manager Liu Xiaowei over for dinner in gratitude to Shell for funding the purchase of guns and vehicles for anti-poaching forces on the Tibetan Plateau. For Shell, Liang represents a perfect funding opportunity. Heir to a renowned intellectual and political family, he has over the last few years become a nationally known media figure. Mentioned in hundreds of news articles every year, Friends of Nature exhibits a media savvy that would put most corporate public-relations executives to shame. As a member of the Chinese People's Political Consultative Congress (CPPCC), Liang himself is also a political figure of real influence.

Political connections are crucial in China's rapidly growing economy. Until recently, protectionism at the local and national levels made access to government officials and support from their staffs essential for companies seeking to break into China's markets. Even now, as regulations are loosened, ordinary business operations often require the assistance of government bureaucrats. The term *guanxi* (connections) defines the way business works in China. For a foreign business figure, a simple public appearance with a Chinese political leader can secure the cooperation of lower-level bureaucrats—including those who process licenses and permits or enforce regulations.

While the Chinese government does not officially allow lobbying, multinational corporations seek meetings with high-level officials to "show and suggest examples of advanced methods of development," as one General Motors executive puts it. Multinational corporations fund useless government projects in order to buy access to local and national officials, a practice known as a *menpiao* (literally, an "entrance ticket").

The Institute of Human Ecology (IHE) exemplifies the way corporations are using environmental groups to gain political access and promote their public images. In 1996, Dianne Chang founded IHE to "provide leadership in the search for creative solutions to human concerns." With the help of her father, former Vice Premier and Defense Minister Zhang Ai Ping, Ms. Chang organized a board of directors consisting mostly of retired government officials. IHE concentrated its initial efforts on organizing the 1997 China Conference on Environment and Sustainability, the first NGO-organized environmental conference in China.

The mission of the conference was "to provide practical guidance on the technical, legal, fiscal and regulatory challenges of incorporating environmental principles into Chinese development plans, and gain from the lessons of international corporate experience in implementing sustainable development." Organizers understood from an early stage, however, that IHE's strength lay in government connections and political influence—not in leadership or knowledge. IHE openly marketed the conference like any service. "Donors of $100,000 (US) can have breakfast with [then] Premier Li Peng and facilitate a workshop; Donors of $50,000 are official sponsors and get the chance to discuss policy with a wide array or top Chinese leaders."

Not surprisingly, Monsanto and four other environmentally unfriendly multinational corporations each donated $100,000. In addition, each sponsor organized and facilitated a session on an environmental issue. Monsanto defined sustainable agriculture for Premier Li Peng, Natural Resource Committee Chair Qu GePing, several other ministers and vice-premiers, and numerous officials from the State Environmental Protection Agency (including SEPA Director Xie, a classmate to Dianne

Change). To attend the conference, other "concerned environmentalists," including DuPont, Dow, Mitsubishi, Procter and Gamble, and British Petroleum paid sums of either $100,000, $50,000, or $25,000 depending on what level of government access they required. Income from the conference totaled nearly $1 million. Nonprofit organizations have also gotten into the menpiao: The Nature Conservancy sponsored the conference as its "ticket" to start a forest protection project in southwest China.

Financing Needs

Foreign capital inflows and economic growth have not been geographically even in "liberalizing" China—creating great wealth disparities both between the country's Eastern coastal provinces and the rest of the country, and within the most rapidly growing areas. At a time when the Chinese environmental movement must transition into broader environmental and social issues, corporations are filling the environmental funding void—and heading off what could be a challenge to their place in the new China.

Dependency on polluting corporations for funding has already compromised environmental enforcement in many areas of China. Under China's new free-market mentality, almost everything must become self-financed, including environmental regulation. China's Ninth Five-Year Plan allocates $787 million for environmental protection from 1996 to 2000. Only 30%, however, comes from government allocations, while 40% relies on fees from polluting enterprises. According to Jennifer Ehrlich of the *South China Morning Post*, "In the growth-frenzied business climate of the Pearl River Delta, being an environmental protection official and actually enforcing regulations can cost you your job. Even if environment protection bureaus must rely heavily on polluting industries as a major source of income."

NGOs also depend on corporations for their funding. Unfortunately, Chinese environmentalists almost universally see corporate funding as a win-win proposition. "Taking money from corporations is not bad," believes Shelly Shi, one of China's most outspoken and committed environmentalists and co-founder of the Yunnan Conservation Association. "By working with large corporations we can both benefit and change their behavior."

Capitalism is relatively new to China. People accustomed to life under communism are often not aware of the shortcomings in capitalism and the nature of profit-seeking behavior. Since the public has a generally positive view of foreign companies, corporate sponsorship provides not only money for environmental organizations but also the credibility for which many independent environmentalists strive. Liang's invitation to appear as a guest speaker for a Fortune 500 conference in Shanghai last fall enhanced his stature as a political leader in China.

What the environmental movement fails to understand is the size and inertia of multinational corporations. The public relations personnel who make funding decisions have little or no say in other management decisions. While corporations gain political access and influence through their relationships to environmental groups, the same cannot be said of the environmentalists. No Chinese NGO currently comes close to changing the behavior of any large multinational corporation.

Environmentalists in the U.S. are themselves far from immune to the lure of corporate funding. Multinational corporations have representatives on the boards of most of the largest U.S. environmental organizations, often asserting a "softening" influence on programs and activities. With the shift from national to grassroots environmental organizing in the U.S., this trend has started to change. However, Chinese environmentalists, only recently exposed to profit-seeking multinational corporations, have not yet been exposed to the counter-argument. The only Western environmental organizations that have so far been allowed to operate in China are the World Wide Fund for Nature (formerly the World Wildlife Fund) and the Nature Conservancy—both large recipients of petroleum money.

Before 1998, both Friends of Nature and Global Village of Beijing refused funding from Shell and DuPont, despite repeated offers. Friends of Nature President Liang Congjie and Global Village President Sherri Liao were both skeptical about receiving money from large international polluters. In fall 1997, however, the World Wide Fund for Nature (WWF) organized an event for British Petroleum to present its environmental programs to Chinese environmentalists. This encounter erased Liang's remaining skepticism. Both Friends of Nature and Global Village, facing mounting financial pressures and the difficulties associated with applying for and administering foundation money, followed WWF's lead and accepted grants from Shell.

Like in the U.S., corporate funding has had a "softening" effect on China's environmental organizations. Over the last four years, environmental activism has become almost commonplace in China. The State Environmental Protection Agency estimates that China now has over 2,000 registered environmental NGOs. The Chinese environmental movement, however, has largely focused on "safe issues," says Nick Young, publisher of China Brief, a NGO resource newsletter based in Beijing. Safe territory includes nature conservation and general "environmental awareness" campaigns (children's education, teacher training, etc.). So far, the movement has shied away from an environmental critique of current development models or the distributional analysis of environmental issues.

This is not a new phenomenon in the region. One only needs to look as far as Hong Kong to see how corporate partnerships have affected environmental activism. According to an essay by On-Kwok Lai (et al.) in *Asian Environmental Movements,* large corporations in Hong Kong use funding specifically as a means to soften or moderate the political campaigns and programmatic goals of environmental organizations. "In most cases environmental NGOs have had to realign their mode of operation in accordance with the wishes of corporate sponsors. … Proclaimed in the name of environmental management, private sector initiatives are usually a strong rallying force against progressive environmental policy initiatives."

Environmentalists in mainland China have not been prominent in demanding improved public transportation, urban planning which does not privilege high-consuming elites (e.g., motorists), increased popular participation in the planning process, or compensation from corporations where environments have been destroyed. The HeBei Committee for the Advancement of the Environment, Tsing Hua University (Beijing) Architecture Lecturer Fang Ke, and Yunnan Conservation Association founder Xi Zhinong have all begun to criticize the short-sighted urban "development" policies of the central government and foreign investors. The well-funded national environmental organizations, however, have so far failed to address these issues seriously. "Naturally, China is not the kind of society where one can speak one's mind too stridently," says Nick Young. "But … these issues need to creep onto the agenda, however politely, if China's environmental movement is ever to become the Tiger we hope for …"

If not corporate funding, then what?

Despite the negative consequences, Chinese NGOs depend on corporate funding. Very few foreign foundations give money in China, and when they do, many Chinese NGO leaders feel that application and reporting procedures are too cumbersome to follow. The Chinese economy has not yet developed enough wealth of its own to create an indigenous sector of philanthropy, and Chinese law has no structure to support one.

In the U.S., organizations like Greenpeace have turned to broad grassroots fundraising as an alternative to corporate funding or a reliance on foundations. In China, however, current income levels are too low to support such a strategy. It is also difficult for Chinese environmental organizations to forego money and rely instead on large numbers of member-volunteers. The ruling Chinese Communist Party remains uneasy about non-governmental organizations that claim too large a following. Organizations like Friends of Nature have therefore been reluctant to grow, fearing unnecessary tensions with the government.

Dedicated activists outside major financial centers, such as Wang Mingying, president of Mothers for Environmental Protection, have few options for funding. Last year, through her work at the Shanxi Province Women's Federation, where she serves as the outreach director, Wang raised some money from two maternity-care product companies. In exchange for the sum of 5,000RMB (about US$610) Wang allowed Kaimi Corporation to place an advertisement in her environmental education materials. In tears of despair she recounted how the company refused to pay after the materials had already been printed, leaving her in debt with nowhere to go. Local government agencies reluctantly made up the cost. With few alternatives, Wang would welcome a large multinational that would actually pay for its advertisements.

Seven years ago, Chinese environmentalism began with a few progressive thinkers. It looked like the start of a powerful movement for social change. Many environmental NGOs outside Beijing, including Xi Zhinong and Shi Lihong's Yunnan Conservation

Association, continue to pursue exciting projects, acting as agents of political reform. Unless alternative funding sources—like international foundations—step into the funding void, however, they may eventually be driven into corporate arms, as other environmentalists have been. The Chinese environmental movement is still small, young, and diverse. But the clock is ticking on its youthful exuberance.

FILIPINO DUMP ACTIVISTS TURN WASTE INTO WEALTH

EUGENIO GONZALES AND LIZ STANTON

November/December 2004

To visitors from outside, the Payatas dumpsite outside Manila is at best an eyesore and at worst a vision of hell on Earth. For the thousands of families who earn their livelihoods by recycling materials in Payatas, though, garbage is a form of wealth. "In good times, we can earn more than twice the minimum wage of factory workers just by picking through the garbage," says Zaldy Arevan, an officer of the Payatas Scavengers Association.

Metro Manila is the Philippines' largest urban center, with a growing population of over 10 million. In recent years, four dumpsites—Smokey Mountain, Carmona, Payatas, and San Mateo—have served the metropolis. One by one these sites have been closed, mainly because they were filled beyond their capacity. In early 2001, the last one, the San Mateo landfill, was closed following protests from nearby residents. They had had enough of the stench of the garbage and the daily rumbling of heavy garbage trucks that polluted the air and damaged their roads.

Mountains of garbage piled up on city streets as the 16 Metro Manila municipalities were left to fend for themselves. Illegal dumpsites sprang up in rural areas, endangering the water supply and the health of both rural and urban communities. The re-opening of the Payatas dumpsite and the opening of a new landfill in Rodriguez Town outside of Metro Manila have eased the situation, at least temporarily.

The Ecological Solid Waste Management Act, signed into law in early 2001 at the urging of activists, NGOs, and sympathetic government officials, has encouraged recycling as one response to the landfill crisis. Of the 5,350 metric tons of waste generated daily in Metro Manila in the late 1990s, only 6% was being recycled. Thanks to the new law, the recycling rate now may have reached 15%, according to estimates by the Washington, D.C.-based Earth Day Network.

The Payatas Dump

Payatas, the country's largest open dumpsite, occupies 50 acres in Quezon City, the largest city in Metro Manila. Despite its lack of required liners and piping systems, it receives around 1,200 tons of trash per day. Since the mid-1970s when Payatas started operating, hundreds and later thousands of waste-pickers migrated to work and to live in the dump. They stayed in shacks—usually made from recycled wood, roofing materials, and cardboard—with no access to roads, water, or electricity. In exchange for votes, politicians slowly gave the waste-pickers access to basic utilities, but even today very few have title to their homes.

Roughly 6,000 waste-pickers make or supplement their livings by combing through this mountain of garbage. Families living on the margins of the dump sort out plastics, bottles, metal, and other materials to sell to junk shops that consolidate the recyclables and deliver them to factories for reprocessing. "They work in unsanitary and dangerous conditions but they have no other alternative livelihood," says Celia Tuason of the Vincentian Missionaries Social Development Foundation, an NGO that has worked in Payatas for more than 10 years.

When garbage trucks arrive at the dumpsite entrance, young boys jump onto the back of each truck to pick quickly through the load. These boys, called "jumpers," are hired by junk shop owners to do this work. Inside the entrance, hundreds of waste-pickers wait. They are called "*mangangalahig*," after the pointed tool called a *kalahig* that they use to pick through the garbage. They assemble behind the truck and immediately sift through the garbage as it falls off. They have mastered the art of avoiding being buried by the garbage or run over by the truck, but accidents sometimes happen.

Women and elderly scavengers who lack the physical abilities of the jumpers and the *mangangalahigs* are forced to rely on more tedious but less competitive ways to pick through the waste. They go to areas of the dump that are being leveled by bulldozers, in hope that plastics or metals will be unearthed that may still be of value. There are fewer waste-pickers, and consequently less competition, in these locations, but these workers—called "*suros*," a local term for dredging—face the added risk of being run over by the bulldozers.

The final stage of waste picking is performed by the "*sala*," literally, "to sift through." They go to the areas of the dump that have already been burned or are still burning. Using tongs, the workers sift through the ash looking for metal and other items of value. Others extract clumps of burnt garbage and use nearby waterways to remove the ash, hoping to find useful items. This least rewarding job in the dumpsite is also the riskiest: their chances of recovering items of much value are slim, and the *sala* are constantly subjected to smoke and flames.

On July 10, 2000, more than 200 waste-pickers lost their lives when a huge section of the garbage mountain collapsed after strong rains. Most of those who died were *salas* buried under smoldering garbage. After the accident, the government promptly closed the site. A few months later, however, the dump was re-opened at the request of the waste-pickers themselves, although the collapsed section has been permanently closed. The tragedy attracted more NGOs and government agencies to provide health care and other kinds of assistance to the Payatas scavengers, but their lives remain difficult, and the future of the site is still in question.

The Promised Land

In 1993, the Vincentian Missionaries Social Development Foundation started a savings and credit program for the scavengers of the Payatas dumpsite. The foundation's program catered mainly to women, using a modified Grameen Bank microloan approach that emphasized savings rather than outside funding as a source of capital. Borrowers founded a people's organization, the *Lupang Pangako* (or "Promised Land") Urban Poor Association, Inc. (LUPAI).

From initial seed capital of $2,000 in government funds, LUPAI now manages around $300,000 in savings accounts for its 7,000 members. Today, many LUPAI members engage in micro-enterprises such as small stores, junk shops, and metalworking, which provide goods and services to the scavengers and other local residents. In addition to the revolving credit program, LUPAI has piloted a community mortgage program through which some of its members have acquired ownership of the land where their houses stand. The program has also provided funds for improving streets and water systems. "I have seen how much they have improved their lot in spite of the difficulties and the little help that we could give them. This inspires me to carry on with my work," says Celia Tuason of the Vincentians.

In addition, LUPAI works with other organizations, like the Payatas Scavengers' Association, to improve the living conditions around the dumpsite. As a result of their advocacy, roads leading up to and inside the dump have been improved, and utilities like water and electricity have been provided to the scavengers' homes.

As the Payatas case shows, waste recycling can contribute to poverty reduction. A 1996 survey of waste-picker households in Payatas found that families earned an average of $175 per month, or 20% more than the legislated minimum wage. In addition to cash income, the dump provides some free household goods, such as building materials, furniture, and clothes. The scavengers lack secure rights to access the waste stream, though: they could be "evicted" from the dumpsite at any time because they have no title to the land. In addition, the scavengers' income has fallen as upstream recycling has increased with government regulation and incentives. Whereas in previous years a scavenger typically earned $8 per day, now he or she is lucky to earn $3 per day. Some scavengers, seeing an opportunity, have already banded together to collect garbage upstream, before it arrives at the dump. For a fee, they collect garbage from homes, offices, and malls. This provides additional income to their sorting and recycling activities.

Still, the financial cost of handling solid waste in Metro Manila is estimated to be around $56 per ton. The scavengers, therefore, provide a vital environmental and cost saving service by removing an estimated 65 tons of recyclables per day from the waste stream. If they were paid by the government for the savings they provide, they could earn roughly $3,600 per day, or $1.3 million a year. This would be equivalent to 30% of the average yearly income of all the waste pickers in Payatas—a significant boost to families barely eking out a living at the site.

By treating trash as an asset, the scavengers of Payatas not only secure livelihoods, but also help the Philippines to solve its garbage crisis. If the control and eventual closure of municipal dumpsites like Payatas leads to the proliferation of illegal dumpsites across the country, both the environment and public welfare will suffer. If, instead, creative strategies are adopted by groups like LUPAI, and the government, the crisis could be turned into an opportunity to advance the twin goals of environmental protection and poverty reduction.

The central aim of the Natural Assets Project is to promote creative thinking internationally about strategies to advance simultaneously the goals of poverty reduction, environmental protection, and environmental justice. See <www.naturalassets.org>.

CHAPTER 6

CHANGING THE SYSTEM, CHANGING HOW WE LIVE

NOT THE OWNERS OF THE EARTH

CAPITALISM AND ENVIRONMENTAL DESTRUCTION

An Interview with John Bellamy Foster

SKIP BARRY

March/April 2003

The success of the environmental movement in raising public consciousness can be seen and felt almost on a daily basis. From local recycling efforts to tighter automobile inspection standards, we are constantly reminded of environmental issues. Daily newspapers and nightly newscasts shower us with issues as varied as global warming, the plight of lobsters, and Arianna Huffington's recent attacks on SUVs. For many of us, this may all get a bit overwhelming.

Fortunately, John Bellamy Foster takes a step back and uncovers the connecting threads that tie together these diverse questions. Touching on history, economics, ecology, and philosophy, Foster delves seriously into the complexity and vast scale of today's environmental problems. He also reminds us that many of today's reforms treat the symptoms rather than curing the disease—which is capitalism itself.

Foster is coeditor of *Monthly Review: An Independent Socialist Magazine* and a professor at the University of Oregon at Eugene. His books on society and ecology (including *The Vulnerable Planet: A Short Economic History of the Environment*, *Marx's Ecology: Materialism and Nature*, and *Ecology Against Capitalism*), as well as numerous articles on these issues, have provided those concerned about the environment with a critical analytical foundation for thinking about and acting on today's environmental crisis. Here, he takes on the largest and most pressing environmental and economic issues in a conversation with *Dollars & Sense*'s Skip Barry.

***D&S*: Since Earth Day in 1970 the environmental movement has been successful in raising public awareness of the plight of the environment. To what extent has it been successful in winning environmental protections and more ecological forms of economic development?**

JBF: Environmentalists have scored a lot of important victories over the last three decades. However, this has not prevented the environmental crisis as a whole from getting much worse. One difficulty is that those environmental problems that are easiest to fix within the present system (such as the elimination of lead in gasoline) get addressed, while others that go against the grain of the system, like reducing carbon dioxide emissions, continue on without amelioration. Another difficulty is that the scale and complexity of environmental problems keep on increasing along with the scale and complexity of the world economy—and indeed new problems not previously imagined keep on arising. If you look back three decades to the period following the first Earth Day and compare it to today you will notice two things: First, most of the issues raised at that time, such as the role of toxins in our environment, are still with us, and more often than not on a much larger scale. Second, new problems have arisen that were scarcely on the radar screen thirty years ago—or problems that we recognized then have been qualitatively transformed and present themselves to us now in new forms.

We are still faced with the issue of pesticides raised by Rachel Carson in *Silent Spring* (See "Industry Attacks on Dissent" in Chapter 2). Although a few of the worst pesticides, such as DDT, were banned for use in the rich countries, we now produce in the United States several times the quantity of pesticides that we did when Rachel Carson raised the alarm and most such chemicals are effectively untested and unregulated for their effects on humans.

But if the old environmental problems continue to haunt us, new ones have arisen that are equally or more threatening. Global warming and depletion of the ozone layer were not threats that one heard about commonly within the environmental movement in the early 1970s. Species extinction was often raised but the idea that we were entering a period of the "sixth extinction," in which the extinction rate would rise to a minimum of 1000 times the background (or normal) rate—comparable to the five great mass extinctions in the history of the planet (the most recent being the destruction of the dinosaurs 65 million years ago)—that was not something that was or could have been foreseen on the first Earth Day.

The Worldwatch Institute talks about the "acceleration of history" where the environment is concerned. This acceleration is the product of the exponential growth of an unsustainable economic system, which now operates on a scale that rivals the basic biogeochemical processes of the planet. For example, carbon dioxide is not a pollutant. It is part of our own respiratory system. But when hundreds of millions of cars are driven trillions of miles per year, all pumping carbon dioxide into the atmosphere, the scale of human economic activity becomes of planetary significance, changing the balance within the biosphere. When one considers that a 3% annual rate of growth in world output means a doubling in the size of the economy every twenty five years, so that the size of the world economy would increase by sixteen times in a century, 250 times in two centuries, and 4,000 times in three centuries—it becomes clear that the main reason for what environmentalists call the "acceleration of history" is the exponential growth of the economy itself. China has the highest rate of economic growth in the world at present and this is fueling expectations about its future energy demands. The U.S. Department of Energy has estimated that China's demand for petroleum will increase by almost 1000% between 1997 and 2020.

***D&S*: The Bush Administration rejected an already watered down version of the Kyoto Protocol on global warming. Is the United States government the main barrier to adequately addressing environmental reform?**

JBF: There is no doubt that the United States is the single most important political entity blocking environmental reform. The U.S. refusal to ratify the Kyoto Protocol was a major blow to the struggle against global warming. But this response was virtually inevitable given that the giant corporations were strongly opposed to the climate treaty. The Kyoto Protocol required the United States to reduce its greenhouse gas emissions to 7% below the 1990 level. But U.S. carbon dioxide emissions have actually risen by as much as 18% since 1990. The Clinton administration declared in 2000 that the United States would have to cut its carbon dioxide emissions by up to 30% if it were to meet its meet its targeted reductions under the Kyoto Protocol by 2010. This was viewed as potentially catastrophic by the vested interests (for example, the corporate lobbying group the Global Climate Coalition), since U.S. wealth and power is built around the auto-petroleum complex. The Clinton administration therefore made no attempt to ratify the Kyoto Protocol and did everything it could do to water down and escape the agreement. The Bush administration has simply been more honest in rejecting the climate treaty outright.

***D&S*: How has mainstream economics traditionally dealt with the environment? Does the mainstream perspective lend support to U.S. policies on issues like global warming?**

JBF: Traditionally, mainstream economics has scarcely dealt with the environment at all. Neoclassical economists construct abstract models which treat the economy as a total system that does not exist within a larger biosphere. When environmental problems, such as pollution, have come up economists have traditionally viewed these as "externalities"—essentially outside the private market, falling on society as a whole. Nowadays, however, there are a lot of attempts by neoclassical economists to bring environmental problems within their models. This usually starts with the view that there are "market imperfections" that prevent the system from adequately valuing nature. For example, society has created "market imperfections" in the area of fresh water by treating water as a free good, leading to an imbalance of demand and supply and hence growing water shortages. From a mainstream standpoint this points to the need to have the entire environment brought within the price system. A book was published a number of years ago by leading environmental economists entitled, significantly, Pricing the Planet. The environment is conceived as if it is a set of commodities with prices or values (awaiting to be discovered) that allow for its incorporation into the logic of the self-regulating market system. Of course, most of this is bogus since the natural environment cannot be reduced to commodities to be bought and sold on the market. But various ways of artificially imposing prices on nature have been tried.

Mainstream economists actually believe that in doing all of this they are seriously tackling environmental problems. If nature is incorporated into market relations, they contend, this will solve nearly all ecological problems. It is only economists, however, who believe this. One of the continual sources of frustration for orthodox economists applying this kind of analysis is that the population stubbornly refuses to view everything in nature as having a price tag or as constituting a salable commodity.

With respect to global warming, mainstream economists have taken the issue seriously up to a point. But they tend to underestimate the costs associated with it (since they perceive only the direct costs to the market) and are critical of measures that attempt to cut emissions, such as the Kyoto Protocol, which they see as too costly. William Nordhaus, the most famous establishment economist to address this problem extensively, argues that rather than supporting the Kyoto Protocol and attempting to control emissions the United States should opt for some kind of grand technological solution, like carbon sequestration, designed to increase carbon absorption by the oceans. The fact that such technologies don't exist doesn't seem to matter.

There is a tragic-comic aspect to this. A decade ago atmospheric scientists objected to an article that Nordhaus wrote for Science magazine in which he claimed that the losses to U.S. GDP over the next century as a result of global warming would be on the order of 1%. In response to these criticisms, Nordhaus admitted that he had not taken into account losses in nonmarket sectors, such as the costs associated with the loss of wetlands or a rise in species extinctions. He therefore went on to carry out a survey of a select group of economists and natural scientists on their estimates of the costs to the world economy associated with various global warming scenarios. When he raised the scenario of a 6°C (10.8°F) rise in the earth's average temperature by 2090 (within the range of what the UN Intergovernmental Panel on Climate Change currently believes possible) most conventional economists that he surveyed thought it would have an impact on the Gross World Product of only a few percent. In contrast, natural scientists who were asked about the effect of the same increase in global temperature generally thought it catastrophic, with losses to world economic output ranging from several percent all the way up to 100% (since one scientist assigned a 10% chance to the virtual destruction of all civilization). Nordhaus concluded that those who knew most about the economy were optimistic. Stephen Schneider, a leading atmospheric scientist, retorted that those who knew most about the planet were worried.

***D&S*: Does the environmental crisis call into question the sustainability of capitalist development?**

JBF: The questioning of capitalism is omnipresent in the ecological critique. That is why I entitled my latest book *Ecology Against Capitalism*. Capitalism is all about the accumulation of capital. The commodification of nature in the service of accumulation involves the systematic disruption of spatial and temporal relations that are integral to a sustainable system. It frequently means not just the exploitation of nature but the robbing or pillage of the biosphere. I have tried over the years to find a way of conceptualizing the damaging effects that capitalism has on the environment. In *The Vulnerable Planet* I looked at how capital accumulation conflicts with Barry Commoner's four informal "laws" of ecology: (1) everything is connected to everything else, (2) everything must go somewhere, (3) nature (i.e. evolution) knows best, and (4) nothing comes from nothing. Capitalism, I argued, has its own built-in anti-ecological tendencies: (1) the only lasting connection between things is the cash nexus, (2) it doesn't matter where something goes (how it is externalized) as long as it doesn't reenter the circuit of capital, (3) the self-regulating market knows best, and (4) nature's bounty is a free gift to the property owner.

Recently I concluded that the most powerful way of understanding capitalism's destructive relation to the environment is in terms of what Marx called the "metabolic rift"—or the material estrangement of human beings from the natural conditions and processes that form the bases of their existence. (Marx's concept of metabolic rift is discussed in detail in my book *Marx's Ecology*.) Such a rift occurs when the circulation of commodities and exchange under capitalism ruptures the basic processes governing the circulation of matter and energy—the biogeochemical interactions on which ecosystems and the biosphere depend. For example, prior to growth of modern agribusiness livestock was raised on farms where it provided fertilizer for crops. This is of course part of an ecological cycle stretching back over the ages. Now, however, cattle are forced into giant feedlots and their manure, which cannot under these circumstances be used to fertilize the soil, collects in huge amounts and gives off methane gas, which has become a major factor in global warming.

***D&S*: The "command" economies of the former USSR and Eastern Europe were environmental disasters. Why were they such failures ecologically? What would**

sustainable non-capitalist economies have to look like?

JBF: I don't think that the environmental destruction in the Soviet Union and Soviet-type economies was due mainly to their being "command" economies (although the fact that they were societies that were not socialist in the sense of being controlled by the direct producers was a major factor in their demise). The key here is that the Soviet Union was what is called, in economic terms, a "war economy." It not only operated with little or no excess capacity or unemployment, but it also overdrafted labor and resources. In the resource realm the Soviet Union attempted to extract energy and materials at maximum rates and to absorb them into production in order to promote the maximum short-term economic growth. It soon however came up against the limitations, many of them environmental, to such a strategy. It also got dragged into the massive use of toxic chemicals, nuclear power, giant dams and the like. Part of this tragedy was that in the Cold War context the Soviet Union was trying to compete militarily and economically with the United States, a much bigger economy, and was doing so in a state of constant crisis. According to the principles of mutual assured destruction (MAD) they needed thousands of missiles to point at the United States to counter the thousands of missiles pointed at them, along with all the other paraphernalia of destruction. Consequently, they were unable to use their resources rationally.

The result was a kind of "ecocide" in the Soviet Union, as many observers have noted. However, we tend to be less aware of our own ecocide. Global warming, the destruction of the ozone layer, the elimination of tropical forests, the mass extinction of species, etc.—the panoply of planetary ecological problems that now threaten all life on earth—were not problems produced by the Soviet Union but by the capitalist world economy, which has been far more destructive overall.

The question of how we can create a sustainable economy is obviously difficult to answer. We know a lot of the things that have to be done—the elimination of nuclear power, the shift to solar power, drastic cutbacks in carbon emissions, reductions in throughput of energy and materials, less reliance on toxic chemicals, preservation of natural habitat, etc. But to effect these changes we need to break away from an economic system dedicated to the accumulation of capital by means of the exploitation of labor and the natural environment. It is necessary to abandon those conditions that guarantee unsustainability on a planetary scale.

Marx said that the labor process can be defined as the metabolic relation between human beings and nature. He argued that socialism/communism necessitated that the direct producers rationally regulate this metabolic relation, in harmony with both human needs and the eternal nature-imposed conditions of production. "Even an entire society, a nation, or all simultaneously existing societies taken together," he wrote, "are not owners of the earth, they are simply its possessors, its beneficiaries, and have to bequeath it in an improved state to succeeding generations, as boni patres familias [good heads of the household]." Marx argued that we need to focus on reciprocity, demanding in many cases "restoration." For example, in our relation to the soil those vital elements that are taken away (in this case essential soil chemicals) must be put back. Engels, in line with Marx, was already arguing in the nineteenth century that capitalism had led to the "squandering of our reserves of energy, our coal, ore, forests, etc." He raised the issue of climate change, including rising temperatures, as a result of the destruction of forests.

***D&S*: Since lower-income people worldwide are disproportionately affected by adverse environmental conditions, it seems that the environmental movement must incorporate issues such as class, race, and the third world. To what extent have environmental movements done this? How do you think this can be achieved?**

JBF: Within the environmental movement itself, which is really a collection of movements, the most vital element since the late 1980s has been the "environmental justice" movement—or that part of the movement that sees environmental degradation as inseparably connected to issues of class, race, gender, and international oppression. Leadership in this realm has come from those fighting environmental racism. But ecofeminists have also made crucial contributions. The anti-toxic movement as a whole has had a working class base. And more and more there is a globalization of the environmental struggle that recognizes the reality of ecological imperialism. It was this growth of the environmental justice movement, and the way that it has altered environmental struggles, that allowed environmentalists and labor activists to come together in Seattle in 1999 and in subsequent anti-globalizations struggles. I think that this is the tendency of the future. Capitalism in its relentless commodification and accumulation is breaking down all the barriers. Exploitation, once understood to be centered in factory labor, is now universalized. The earth itself has been brought within the factory, so to speak. In this context all struggles become one.

ACHIEVING THE GOOD LIFE

ADAPTED FROM *GRACEFUL SIMPLICITY: TOWARD A PHILOSOPHY AND POLITICS OF SIMPLE LIVING*

JEROME M. SEGAL

July/August 1999

The recent enthusiasm for "simple living" in the United States is largely apolitical, with acolytes maintaining that ours is an affluent society, whose central problem is an unenlightened consciousness. An entire self-help literature has blossomed in the last decade, showing people how they can live well with vastly lower income. Certainly, there is some truth to the idea that we need to be liberated from our ever expanding sense of what constitutes a necessity. However, our biggest problem is not warped perceptions at the individual level, but extreme inefficiency at the structural level: fundamental human needs can be met only with high levels of income.

Simple living, espoused by individuals and groups as diverse as Gandhi, Thoreau and the Quakers, can be most easily defined by what it is not. At its core, the simple living philosophy is that "the good life" is not achieved through ever increasing getting-and-spending. Those rejecting the dominant American dream on an individual level may focus on friends, lovers, and family, or religion, or art and literature, or political struggle, or service to others, or the pursuit of knowledge.

A politics of simplicity—focused at the societal level—is similarly broad-based. Rather than promoting one particular way of life, it promotes a society in which people with even modest incomes can have the freedom to engage in fundamental projects beyond merely making a living. Rather than evaluating economic progress in terms of an ever-expanding cornucopia of goods and services, a politics of simplicity measures economic progress by how well core economic needs are being met and whether leisure time is expanding.

Over the last hundred years, satisfying certain basic needs has become much cheaper, while others have sky-rocketed in cost. The number of work hours the average person in the United States must devote to meeting their needs for food and clothing has fallen dramatically. In 1900, food and clothing constituted 56% of the household budget; today it is 20%. Meanwhile, costs for housing, transportation, health care, education and child care have increased. "Need required income" (income required to meet our needs) has gone up markedly.

In many critical ways, this shift is not the result of rising standards. In fact, we have lowered our expectations. Take the example of housing—the largest component of the average household budget. Certainly, the typical middle class house has changed dramatically, from having an outhouse to indoor plumbing to multiple bathrooms. Still, for most American families, the key to choosing housing is not the physical house, but the neighborhood: not too far from work and services, with access to good public schools, and safe enough for children to play outside. This standard is increasingly out of reach of moderate income families. In the Washington, DC area where I live, houses in such a neighborhood cost upward of $250,000. The solution is not higher incomes; more effective demand would only push prices higher. The real issue is supply, but not in the physical sense. We need to make existing urban neighborhoods viable places to live.

Consider transportation. One hundred years ago transportation represented 3% of the household budget. Today the figure is 19%. We have built a suburbanized society with extremely limited public transportation. A car is a necessity in most areas—families with two wage earners generally need two of them. Reducing household expenditures on transportation requires greater investment in public transport and the design of a simple living automobile: one that is safe, inexpensive, long lasting and can be repaired by anyone handy with tools.

Education is another key example. In the nineteenth century the battle for free public education was waged and won. Free public schooling through high school became the norm nationwide. Relatively few people went to college. The vast majority of jobs required only high school education. Today, access to most interesting work requires a college education, and often an advanced degree. Costs reach $30,000 per year. One hundred years ago, free education provided you with a viable point of entry into the economy. Today, it provides access to very little: only a small number of jobs available with a high school education provide a living wage. We could take major steps in this area with surprisingly limited funds. For $25 billion annually we could eliminate virtually all tuition at state universities for both undergraduate and graduate education. In an $8 trillion economy, this is only a fraction of our annual expenditures.

To make simple living an option for all, a politics of simplicity must go beyond reducing cost of meeting core needs and address a living wage for all, education for simple living, and increased leisure time.

From the mid-1800s until the Great Depression, reduction in work time was a central criterion of economic progress. Work time decreased from 70 hours to 40 hours per week. In 1933 legislation mandating a 30 hour work week passed the U.S. Senate, but died in the House. In recent years, fuller participation by married women in the formal workforce has led to an explosion in total family work time. We need to take the benefits of productivity growth and divide them between higher incomes and increased leisure time, like earlier generations did. Here is one possibility: add 16 three-day weekends to the ten enjoyed by most workers in this country, giving us a three-day weekend every other week. Introduced at the rate of two new holidays a year for the next eight years, this would reduce work time about 1% a year. With productivity growth around 2%, this would still allow for marginally higher incomes.

None of the policies I propose here are truly radical. They could be accomplished through ordinary politics and the creative use of referenda. What is radical is what lies behind them: a recognition of the limited place of money in the good life and a commitment to making simple living feasible for all.

WHAT AN ENVIRONMENTALLY SUSTAINABLE ECONOMY LOOKS LIKE

THAD WILLIAMSON

July/August 1999

Greens and economic progressives are seen as uncertain, uneasy allies—and perhaps not allies at all. Think of those spotted-owl-loving, middle-class activists clashing with blue collar loggers in the Pacific Northwest. Or the clash between liberal economists who still count progress in terms of jobs created, growth generated, and increases in consumption, and environmental activists who challenge those very ways of measuring progress. "Growth" to these activists is part of the problem, not the solution.

But do green politics necessarily conflict with progressive economic goals? Or can environmental protection live and thrive in a world dedicated to eradicating poverty, nurturing equality and economic security, and the continued advancement of productivity and technology?

In a word, yes. An environmentally "sustainable" economy is one that neither depletes natural resources nor pollutes at levels that overwhelm the ability of ecosystems to absorb waste. Such an economy would almost certainly need to overlap with many of the traditional goals of economic progressives, allowing us to envision an ideal world that is both socially and ecologically sustainable. What would that world look like?

First, it would provide economic security for individuals and communities. So long as most citizens are less than six months' paychecks away from insolvency, and so long as they worry that their income may be taken away, economic expansion (i.e., growth) and job creation will, most of the time and for most people, always be a higher political priority than environmental protection.

The link between economic security and sustainability runs at a deeper level as well. In a highly inegalitarian society such as ours, where the quality of public goods like neighborhood safety and public schools varies widely, individuals and families are pressured not just to subsist, but to earn enough to live an ecology-straining middle-class lifestyle.

At the community level, if localities remain dependent on the investment decisions of private businesses for their economic health, protection of the environment will tend to take a back seat. Just look at the way poor, deindustrialized cities such as Chester, Pennsylvania, court particle-spewing trash incinerators for the modest revenue they provide.

If we want to move to a society in which acquiring more and more goods is not the highest priority for individuals, and "growth" is not the highest priority for most communities, then we need a baseline of economic security.

Second, we must create a sense of self based on something besides consumerism. Of course, economic insecurity is not the only reason Americans are driven to consume at extraordinarily high levels. As Thorstein Veblen first argued in 1899, and as Juliet Schor documented in the 1990s, consumption is often used to mark social status, particularly with regard to goods that can be made visible to one's peers, such as cars, clothes, and lipstick. As workers, most Americans are provided with little scope for individual expressiveness, but as consumers, they feel free to follow their wishes in making decisions—decisions which then form a critical part of American identities. The result is a nation of individuals shaped by a compulsion to consume goods and services, and to increase that consumption over time. By contrast, in an ecologically sustainable society, people's core satisfactions could not come from buying decisions, and they would need to have a sense of when enough is enough.

Third, producers who damage the environment must also bear the costs of their damage. As it stands, private enterprises force the public to pay the costs of their polluting and depletion of natural resources. Since the true costs of production are not reflected in the prices of goods on the market, firms benefit by shifting costs such as pollution cleanup to the public. This system gives businesses an incentive to "externalize" environmental costs off their own balance sheets if they can get away with it—and to resist attempts by governments to minimize the costs through regulation. Advocates of ecological sustainability thus argue that firms should bear the full cost of their activities. A major question, of course, is how to best accomplish this goal.

Fourth, we must also use as much environmentally friendly technology as we can in our new world. Unfortunately, over the course of this century, the U.S. government intervened in the economy to promote ecologically inefficient and destructive economic practices. While giving a pittance to the development of solar and wind power, the government sank about $100 billion of subsidies into nuclear power between 1950 and 1990. Similarly, the government lavished funds upon the Highway Trust Fund and created the interstate highway system while allowing public transit of all types to decay. To this day, over 80% of federal transportation spending supports automobile-related infrastructure, leaving less than 20% for mass transit. Such spending patterns, along with additional subsidies like tax write-offs for home mortgages, help generate suburban sprawl (and thereby exacerbate the ecological damage caused by cars). At the same time, regulators often tackle problems at the "end of the pipe" instead of seeking to change the productive processes themselves.

In any sustainable society, these sorts of choices will need to be reversed and priority given to implementing the most environmentally friendly technology possible. Environmental technology, in fact, could be the source of millions of new jobs in the next century—and jobs building high-speed rail cars would likely pay just as well as jobs making automobiles. Similarly, labor-intensive public work projects could be undertaken in support of ecological goals—to beautify cities, build bike paths, install solar panels, remove lead paint, and insulate buildings. Governments could also aggressively use their purchasing policies to help promote the development of cutting-edge environmentally sound products.

Within the current structure of power, however, the private interests that stand to lose public funds—such as the oil and car companies—thwart any shift in public spending toward more ecologically and socially rational goals and resist any laws that would mandate certain kinds of production processes. They have the money to intervene in elections and (even more importantly) shape legislation—and they are aided by the fact that few politicians are eager to support measures that may damage companies in their districts. Just look at the way the energy lobby thoroughly discredited and defeated Vice President Al Gore's modest proposal for an energy tax in 1993. In contrast, an ecologically sustainable society would require that politics not be dominated by corporate or private interests—a very tough structural requirement rarely mentioned in the conventional policy debate about the environment.

Finally, a world where ecological and progressive economic goals are unified would be one where growth is no longer the top priority. In our corporate capitalist economy, banks and investors consider whether profits and the economy as a whole will grow before sending their capital the way of any business. In contrast, an environmentally sustainable economy would not need high rates of growth to function in a healthy manner. Growth would not be the goal of a sustainable economy, nor would the fair distribution of economic goods depend on continual growth. Instead, with every individual and community guaranteed a stake in the economy, it would not be necessary to focus so much on expanding production. Also, the gains from more efficient production would be distributed to people as reduced work-hours or more stringent environmental protection.

Still, even in a sustainable economy, economic growth per se need not be eliminated entirely. While one way to cut the use of resources and pollution is to cut production and shrink the economy, another is to make productive systems more efficient. We also might choose to produce those goods that cause less ecological damage. There is no inherent reason why a society that commits itself to ecologically efficient production, both in the actual production process and in the kinds of goods created, might not generate what we today call economic growth. For instance, if we decided to hire more elementary school teachers—and at the same time to consume fewer lawn care products—ecological damage would drop even as the size of the economy stayed roughly the same. The difference is that economic growth as a good in itself would not be the central aim of such an economy.

The Institutions of a Sustainable Economy

Ecological problems might be very easy to solve if we imagine an all-powerful state that enforces strict ecological standards on both individuals and businesses. Not only is such a vision unattractive on its own terms, it probably provides only a temporary solution to the ecological problem. Sooner or later, an ecofascist regime that tried to impose sound ecological practices without the support of its citizens would probably be overthrown, leading us back to square one: how to make the goals of democracy, economic justice, and ecological sustainability fit together.

How would that be possible? Is it possible?

At the community level, perhaps the fundamental questions to consider are: Who owns capital?, and, Who gets to make basic decisions over how production is carried out? The usual answers—small businesses, corporations, the government, or workers—would all have the incentive to pollute or use ecologically wasteful production strategies. A fifth possible solution is local community ownership. To see why, it's worth reviewing the shortcomings of the other possible answers.

Styles of regulation that allow private businesses to organize production as they see fit will always face an uphill struggle in trying to get businesses to pay for the ecological costs they generate, a hill that is especially steep in the case of nations like the United States where social democratic politics are weak. Moreover, even the success stories associated with social democratic-style environmental regulation have limitations. For example, no industrialized country has yet succeeded in constraining the growth of the automobile/highway complex, as we must to reduce greenhouse gases.

Worker-owned firms are an attractive solution, it seems, since workers may be less likely to pollute their own communities (or risk their own health in the workplace), and more subtly, because worker-owned firms (as Douglas Booth argues) will have less incentive to grow than capitalist firms. Perhaps, but workers within a given enterprise still may have interests different from the public's. Given the reins of management, workers may come to see ecological responsibility as a threat to the bottom line, as Gar Alperovitz and Herbert Gintis have each suggested—especially if they can send the pollution from their plant downstream or to the next town.

State ownership of firms also poses problems. When government officials are not held accountable and when ecological values are subordinated to other aims, both state-owned enterprises and general government operations are capable of doing disastrous damage to the environment. Even in the most favorable circumstances, public companies may find it rational to compromise the needs of local ecosystems in the name of some larger public interest. At worst, we've seen the Energy Department contaminate desert stretches of Nevada from nuclear weapons tests carried out in the "public interest."

This brings us to a fifth possible answer to the "who should control capital?" question: local-level community ownership. "Community-owned" firms might include municipally owned enterprises, firms owned by nonprofit organizations that represent community interests (such as community development corporations), or companies whose stock can be owned only by local residents (as in Michael Shuman's concept of "community corporation.") In theory, community-owned enterprises are more likely to take full responsibility for the ecological costs of their activity to the degree that they are made accountable to the community. If the managers of a community-owned firm chose to sacrifice ecological goals for the sake of higher production, citizens would have the opportunity, via the political process, to remove them.

Moreover, profits from a community-owned firm could be distributed to citizens as a second income, thus helping to meet the economic security requirement previously noted. And perhaps best of all, there is no threat that a community firm would move away—removing the sword hanging over towns that want tough ecological standards but not at the cost of jobs.

The most widespread form of community ownership in the United States in the

20th century are the roughly 2,000 local-level, nonprofit, public electric utilities, which offer lower rates, more public accountability, and a better (although far from perfect) environmental record than their private counterparts. But many other forms of community ownership have sprouted up in the past two decades as well. These include businesses owned and operated by community development corporations, community land trusts, community-supported agriculture operations, community credit unions, and municipal enterprises.

Community-owned firms, then, would appear to be the best answer to the question of "who should control capital," at least within medium-size and large firms, and the recent growth of various forms of community ownership indicates this is a plausible solution. This does not mean that other forms of ownership need to be obliterated; on the contrary, community-owned firms could coexist along with small businesses, worker-owned firms, joint public-private enterprises, and some larger-scale public enterprises. The key is that the local community must have substantial control over the practices of enough enterprises to anchor the local economy and set a tone for overall production practices.

Community control of land—especially downtown land and undeveloped land—would also be important to optimizing local communities' ecological health. Patterns of land development driven by private developers have resulted in auto-dominated, sprawled out forms of urban development. Community ownership of land would make shifting to ecologically friendly, resource-saving urban designs far more plausible—and rents collected from leases to downtown businesses could also be directly distributed to residents or given to them as services to help solve the economic security problem.

A picture thus emerges of a local economy characterized by a critical mass of community ownership, along with substantial community ownership of land, allowing local level democratic politics to steer firms toward ecological goals and allowing any community dividend to be distributed to citizens (enhancing their economic security). Even if this vision could be achieved with every locality in America, would such an achievement be enough to create a sustainable society?

Hardly. We'd still need mechanisms at the state or perhaps regional level to ensure that one community does not dump on another and meets ecological standards. There would also need to be a planning mechanism to allocate enough capital to each community to guarantee local-level full employment and to help communities adjust when some industries decline due to market shifts.

Governments would also provide important public goods relevant to sustainability, including rail and public transit, development of alternative energy sources, oversight of needed ecological clean-ups, and coordination of the overall macroeconomy. But by essentially removing the private corporation with its disproportionate sway over the political process, and replacing it with firms directly tied to community interests, it ought to be easier to decide how to spend the public works budget, how long the standard work week should be, and so on in an ecologically rational manner.

Continental or global forms of ecological governance may be appropriate on specific ecological issues such as greenhouse gas emissions. (Gar Alperovitz offers an overview along these lines involving economic institutions at the local, regional, and national levels.)

This kind of system would have a far better chance of meeting the needs of a sustainable society than any industrial society that exists now (be it capitalist, social democratic or state socialist.)

But can it be said that this proposed system is inherently sustainable? No—or, at least, not exactly. In fact, it is probably impossible to design a modern economy that could guarantee ecological sustainability while also preserving other crucial norms such as liberty, equality, and democracy. The best we can hope for is an economy that meets the logical prerequisites for a sustainable society and permits citizens to make democratic social choices about what sort of world they wish to live in.

Some citizens may chafe at any state-mandated shifts in their lifestyle and consumption habits (such as one bag of garbage per household per week) while others will believe that the trade off is worth it. The outcome of such political struggles is uncertain, and from time to time the public no doubt would make the wrong choices from a rigorous ecological point of view. But at least such bad choices would be made in the name of the public interest, not in response to private interests or as steps needed to grease the wheels of a growth-oriented economy.

To be sure, in the long interval before a truly sustainable society is built, there will continue to be episodes in which zero sum tradeoffs between the economy and the environment must be made. But those episodes should not blind either greens or economic progressives to the common ground both groups share and will no doubt need to share if either group is to achieve its political aims in the 21st century.

Resources: Ted Howard, "Ownership Matters," (National center for Economic and Security Alternatives, 1999), <www.ncesa.org>; Mark Hertsgaard, Earth Odyssey (Broadway Books, 1999); Gar Alperovitz, "Sustainability and the System Problem," *PEGS Journal*, 1996.

CONTRIBUTORS

Frank Ackerman is Director of Research and Policy at the Global Development and Environment Institute at Tufts University, and a founder of *Dollars & Sense.*

Skip Barry is a former member of the *Dollars & Sense* collective.

Marc Breslow is an economist and former co-editor at *Dollars & Sense.*

Jan Clausen is a faculty member at Eugene Lang College.

Daniel DeLisi lived in China from 1996 to 1998 and co-founded to China-American Chamber of Commerce's Corporate Philanthropy Forum.

Laurie Dougherty is a *Dollars & Sense* associate.

Bob Feldman is a former *Dollars & Sense* collective member.

Daniel Fireside is Book Editor at *Dollars & Sense.*

Ross Gelbspan is a former reporter for the *Boston Globe*. His most recent book is *Boiling Point: How Politicians, Big Oil and Coal, Journalists, and Activists Are Fueling the Climate Crisis.*

Eugenio M. Gonzales is an independent consultant of the International Labor Organization, providing technical and financial assistance to small and medium community-based enterprises.

Lisa Heinzerling is a Professor of Law at Georgetown University Law School, specializing in Environmental Law.

David Holtzman is a former *Dollars & Sense* intern.

David L. Levy is a Professor of Management at the University of Massachusetts - Boston

Toussaint Losier is the Program Coordinator for groundWork USA and a member of the *Dollars & Sense* collective.

Anuradha Mittal established and is executive director of the policy think tank The Oakland Institute.

Kevin Murray is Director of Advocacy and Communications for the Unitarian Universalist Service Committee.

Laura Orlando is executive director of the ReSource Institute for Low Entropy Systems and a member of the *Dollars & Sense* collective.

Project Underground is a Berkeley-based organization that provides informational, technical, legal and scientific support for communities facing abusive oil, gas and mining operations.

William E. Rees is the Director for the School of Community and Regional Planning at the University of British Columbia in Vancouver.

Alejandro Reuss is a Doctorial candidate in economics at the University of Massachusetts - Amherst and a former co-editor and collective member at *Dollars & Sense.*

Peter Rosset is the former co-director of the Food First Institute.

Jonathan Rowe is a senior fellow at Redefining Progress in San Francisco and a contributing editor at the *Washington Monthly.*

Adria Scharf is former co-editor of *Dollars & Sense.*

Samuel Scott is a maritime historian.

Jermone Segal is a philosopher at the University of Maryland's School of Public Affairs.

Liz Stanton is the editorial director for the National Assets Project and teaches economics at the University of Massachusetts-Amherst.

Thad Williamson is an assistant professor for the Jepson School of Leadership Studies at the University of Richmond and a *Dollars & Sense* associate.